The World's Great Sermons

VOLUME VII

HALE TO FARRAR

THE
WORLD'S
GREAT
SERMONS

COMPILED BY

GRENVILLE KLEISER

Formerly of Yale Divinity School Faculty;
Author of " How to Speak
in Public," Etc.

With Assistance from Many of the Foremost
Living Preachers and Other Theologians

INTRODUCTION BY

LEWIS O. BRASTOW, D.D.

Professor Emeritus of Practical Theology
in Yale University

IN TEN VOLUMES

VOLUME VII—HALE TO FARRAR

FUNK & WAGNALLS COMPANY
NEW YORK and LONDON

CONTENTS

VOLUME VII.

CONTENTS

HALE

THE COLONIZATION OF THE DESERT

BIOGRAPHICAL NOTE

EDWARD EVERETT HALE, Congregational-ist divine and author, was born in Boston in 1822. He was graduated at Harvard in 1839 and became a Unitarian preacher in 1846 at Worcester. In 1850 he removed to Boston, where his most important life's work was accomplished as a preacher and writer. A collected edition of his writings, in ten volumes, was published in 1901. His varied literary enterprises and undertakings have been too many to be enumerated here. His most famous work is "The Man Without a Country." He is at present chaplain to the United States Senate.

THE WORLD'S GREAT SERMONS

HALE

BORN IN 1822

THE COLONIZATION OF THE DESERT

*God saw everything that he had made. And behold,
it was very good.*—Gen. i., 31.

THIS simplest expression of the earliest
religion comes back to us with new
force in the midst of all the wonderful
revelations of our modern life.

In ten weeks' time I have crossed from one
ocean to the other; I have crossed backward
and forward over the Allegheny and the Rocky
Mountains and the Sierra Nevada, with the
valleys between them, and the slopes which
rise from the ocean on either side. This means
a journey through twelve of the old thirteen
States and fifteen of the new States and Ter-
ritories. It means intercourse with people of
the North and the South, the Gulf and the
West, the Pacific coast and the mountains. It
means intercourse with the white race, the
black race, the red race, and the Chinaman.
The variety of climate is such that I have wel-
comed the shade of palm-trees, and that I have
walked over snow where it had drifted twenty
feet beneath me. I have picked oranges from
the tree, and camellias from the twig in the

3

open air, and within three hours of good-by to the camellia I was in a driving snow-storm, where the engine drivers were nervous because they had no snow plow. In all this variety I have a thousand times recalled the simplest expression of the oldest words of the Bible: "God saw everything that he had made, and behold, it was very good."

The solid recognition of this truth—not, indeed, in any small sense; but in that sense which is general and comprehensive—is at the bottom of all true religious philosophy. It is not true in any smaller sense. For I cannot say that it is good to be bitten by a mosquito or worried by a fly, if I can escape fly or mosquito. No, that is not true. And I do not suppose that the simple author of this text meant any such extravagance. But this is true, that the world is so made and ordered that man, who is himself a creator—man, who shares the wishes, instincts, and plans of the Power who directs the world—man can take the world in his hands and compel it to serve his nobler purposes.

God saw the world, and he said: "Yes, this is what I want for My home and the home of children who love Me. It is a world very good to them, and they shall subdue it to My purposes." To recognize this, to feel the fitness of the world for man and man's fitness for the world, this is the basis of consistent optimism. Nobody says that the top of the

4

Rocky Mountains is a good place for whales, or that the Ojai Valley is a good place for polar bears; but a consistent optimism says that the world is a good place for man; and it says that man is so closely allied to the God who is the life of the world that he can take the world for his own, and make it his home and his heaven. This consistent optimism is the basis of all sound theology.

It is to be observed, however, that man gains no such control of the world, and the world does not prove fit for man, unless he has found out that he is akin to God and can enter into His work. There is no such victory to the savage, who is afraid of God. So long as he thinks the powers of nature are his enemies, he makes them his enemies. I do not believe the old cave-dwellers, fighting hyenas with clubs, and often finding that they were second-best in the encounter, thought this world the best of worlds. I do not believe that the Digger Indian, who spent his tedious day in rummaging for ants and beetles to eat, and was very happy if he caught a lizard—I do not believe that he said that the world was very good. True, I think both of them had visions and hopes of a better time; but while they were in the abject misery of cold and starvation, that better time had not dawned. It did not dawn because they had not taken on them the dignity and duty of children of God. They were not about their Father's

5

business. They did not see Him nor hear Him, nor in any wise know Him. They did not conceive that they were on His side nor He on theirs. And it is not till man comes up to some comprehension that God has sent him here on an infinite business; that he and the Author of this world are at one in this affair of managing it; it is not till man knows God as his friend and not his enemy, that man with any courage and success takes the business of managing into his own hands. Then is it that he finds what pleasure, nay what dignity, there is in taming the lightning and riding on the storm. And then he knows enough of the divine Being, His purpose and His power, to see that the world is good, and that God should call it good in its creation.

All this forces itself on one's thought as he sees how it is that nature has been pursued and caught and tamed in these mountains and these valleys. For nature is the nymph so wittily described by Virgil. She

"Flies to her woods; but hopes her flight is seen."

Man, so long as he is savage, hates her and fears her. If he worships, it is the abject worship of those who bring sacrifices to buy her favor. And it may be said in passing that the last visible form of pure barbarism or savagery is any theology which supposes that God's favor must be bought by any price paid by man in exchange. When man finds, by any revelation, the conditions of absolute religion, which are simply faith, hope and love, all this is changed. When he looks up to God gladly, looks forward to the future cheerfully, and looks round on the world kindly, he finds, possibly to his surprize, that he is working on the lines God works on, and means to have him work on. Now he is on "his Father's business." While he rows the boat, the tide sweeps the right way. While he stretches the wire, the lightning is waiting and eager to do his errand. And so soon as man the divine appears upon the scene—man the child of God, who knows he shares God's nature—why, easily and quickly the valleys are exalted and the mountains and the hills made low; the deserts blossom as the rose, and even the passing traveler sees that this world was made for man and man for this world. And he understands as he has never understood before what this is, that he himself is of the nature of the God at whose present will this world comes into order. He understands better what the old text means, which says that God is satisfied with the world which He has made.

I crossed the continent westward and eastward on this journey, fresh from recent reading of the history of the first Spanish occupation. What did the Spaniards find there? They found in what we call New Mexico the Zuni cities which, in a sad decline, exist to-day. From those cities Casteneda led a party of Spanish horsemen eastward in search of a certain mythical king who was supposed to have much gold and many jewels. Those adventurous men rode for a whole summer across the prairies and plains which are now Colorado, and Kansas, and Missouri, and struck the Missouri, or perhaps the Mississippi. You know that much of the country is now fertile beyond praise. Mile after mile you can see corn, wheat; wheat, corn; corn, wheat; wheat, corn; and the production to the acre increases year by year. The States through which Casteneda's line of travel passed now number four or five millions of people; and they feed, from their agriculture, say twenty millions more. Now when Casteneda and his people passed and repassed over this region they did not meet a single man. woman or child. They were opprest by the horrible loneliness of their journey. They felt, as Magellan's people felt when they were crossing the Pacific Ocean, with that horrible east wind, with a calm sea before and never a sight of an island or a man. When Casteneda came at last to the Mississippi—or Missouri—they had no heart to build a raft to cross it and incur more such solitude; and they went back the way they came. And the fame of its loneliness was such that no man attempted the adventure for more than a hundred years.

When, in 1682—say a hundred and thirty years after—the great La Salle discovered the Mississippi River, and sailed south upon it, leaving Chicago, crossing Illinois, and so striking the Father of Waters, his experience of this utter loneliness was the same. He touched every night on one shore or the other. He is, therefore, the discoverer of seven of the Western States—States which now feed fifty million people and number seven or eight million of their own. Only twice, I think, did he meet any great body of men. Not five times did he find traces of the hand of man or the foot of man. Through the same solitude he returned; and his report was of a virgin world of elk, and deer, and buffalo; of shrubs and trees, of fish and fowl; but a world without men.

The inference was drawn, hastily, but not unnaturally, that these regions could not sustain men. On the Atlas given me as a boy, the "Great American Desert" covered the greater part of the region west of the Mississippi. It is now the home of the millions I have been enumerating. And in the last map I have seen, the Great American Desert appears as hardly a "speck on the surface of the earth."

The change which I have described has been wrought in the lifetime of people of my age. It is wrought simply and wholly by the passion for emigration which belongs

9

to our own race. In Mr. Hoar's happy phrase, people of our blood "thirst for the horizon."

In the year 1833 De Tocqueville, observing the steadiness of this wave, calculated its average flow as seventeen miles westward every year. That was the rate at which it had moved since the Federal Constitution made it possible. Speaking roughly, there were then two thousand miles of desert between the Missouri River and the Pacific. At De Tocqueville's rate, the wave would have been one hundred and twenty years in reaching that ocean. But it happened that in 1849 the Western coast was settled in the gold discovery. An Eastern wave began which has now met the Western. The two together have founded the great cities—for we must call them so—of the Rocky Mountains.

Now, in the face of that contrast between the last century and this century, one asks why that half of our continent is any more fit for men than it was then. The answer is, that it was not fit for the kind of men on it then; and that the kind of men that have tamed it are the kind of men who were fit for it, and whom it was fit for.

The study of history and of physical geography becomes a study of what we mean by man and man's capacities. California, for instance, was the same country in 1650 that it was in 1850. The south wind blew from the sea, and that, in the north temperate zone, is the great physical requisite. There was as much gold, and quicksilver, and copper, and tin in the mountains as there is now. There was the same soil and the same water on the hillsides. But the men, and women, and children were afraid of their gods; they were afraid of nature; they had neither faith, nor hope, nor love. They had none of the elements of eternal power except as an acorn has the possibilities of an oak.

To these people there came, sooner or later —with the best motives, but still without the essentials of life—fifty families of Franciscan monks. They came, observe, without wives or children. They defied thus the first law of human life, or the life God intends His children to live in. The primitive trinity, from which all false trinities have grown, is the father, the mother and the child. The Franciscan communities were false to all Divine law, if it were only in their failure here.

They gathered around them, by the higher civilization which they brought, great communities of starving Indians. They taught them to feed themselves as they had never been fed before. So far they improved the race, and lifted its civilization above that ant-eating and lizard-chasing of the Digger Indian. But then the Catholic Church, by the necessary subordination of man to the

organized Church, takes man's life out of
him.

> "The day
> That makes a man a slave, takes all his life away."

The words are as true to-day as they were in
Homer's time. Nor is there any sadder instance of it than is the powerlessness of the
tribes of amiable slaves who were collected
under the protection of the Franciscan missions in California, or Jesuit missions in Para-
guay.

The native races between the Pacific and
the Atlantic were dying faster than their children were born. They were dying of the diseases named laziness, ignorance, and war.
They were not subduing the continent. They
were not fit for it, nor it for them. What is
the distinction of the race to which we belong,
that it succeeds where these have failed? The
history of the country accentuates that distinction.

It would be absurd to pretend that the average frontiersman was a man of what are called
saintly habits. Often he was not conscious
that he had any divine errand. But the frontiersman, to whose courage and perseverance
is due that forward wave we study, was a
man. He did not take his opinion or instruction from any priest. There was no one between him and the good God. Often he sought
Him. So far so good. And often he did not

seek Him. That one admits. But he never sought any one else's advice or direction. He was no slave, as the Indian of California was. He was not commissioned by a superior, as the Franciscan priest of the mission was. He was a man. He was independent and he was brave. If he did the right thing, therefore, he succeeded; if he did the wrong thing, why, he failed. And no one else tried just the same experiment. In this first trait of absolute independence he showed the infinite characteristic of a child of God.

Second, and perhaps more important, he took with him his wife and his children. Here is the great distinction of American emigration, which contrasts against the plans of Spaniards or Frenchmen, and of the earlier Englishmen. Historically it begins with the Pilgrims, of whom there were as many Pilgrim mothers as there were Pilgrim fathers. It is of them that Emerson says that "they builded better than they knew."

The frontiersman is independent. He lives with and for his family. And, once more, he is an enthusiast in determining that to-morrow shall be better than to-day. The Indian had no such notion. The Franciscan had not. But this profane, ignorant pioneer had. He believed implicitly in the country behind him and in the future before him. "I tell you, sir, that in ten years you will see in this valley such a city as the world never saw." Profane

13

he may be, ignorant he may be, cruel he may be; but he believes in the idea; he is quickened and goaded forward by an infinite and majestic hope.

Given such conditions, the historical steps are easy. All this is impossible till you have a nation, to give peace and compel peace, so that the separate settler shall know that the whole majesty of the world is behind him. There shall be no abiding quarrel between man and man as to the line of a claim or the title of a mine. The nation shall decide, and its whole majesty shall enforce the decision. Or, if there is any massacre by an Apache or a Blackfoot, the country behind, tho a thousand miles behind, shall stretch forth her arm to avenge that lonely family. This means peace instead of war. All this had to wait, therefore, until the formation of the nation called the United States—the greatest peace society the sun ever shone upon, and the model for societies yet larger. With the birth of that nation, the real Western wave begins.

I do not claim for every pioneer that he thought he went as an apostle of God. But in the emigrant wave from the very beginning, the best blood, the best faith, the best training of the parent stocks have gone. Science has sent her best. The determination for thorough education has planted better school houses in the wilderness than the emigrant left at home. And on Sunday, in a church, one is proud to say that the organized Church of Christ, in the liberty of a thousand communions, has covered with her egis the settler most in advance. He could not keep in advance of the missionary and of his Bible; and, to his credit be it said, he did not want to.

So much for the personnel. Now, speaking roughly, what has been the motive for the great Western wave, which is making this garden out of that desert?

First, there is the passion for adventure, the thirst for the horizon, which drives old Leatherstocking and the men like him away from the haunts of men. This in itself produces nothing. Next and chiefly, the desire to make homes—the noblest desire given to man, and the desire in which he follows the will of God most distinctly and completely. Miners want to strike metals; farmers want to find good soils; fruit men try for climate and irrigation; all with the direct wish to make homes more happy than they have been before.

Again, young men go that they may get forward faster than in old communities—and who can wonder? Men of sense give up the unequal contest with nature in a northern and eastern climate to find a country where nature is on their side. People in delicate health go where they find softer air, more spring and less winter. But no man goes to get rich alone. No man wants to eat gold or to drink it. The wish and hope is to make homes where father, mother and children can live the life which God ordained. These are no Franciscan friars, these are no Apache bandits, to whom has been given the subjugation of a continent. Side by side with the pioneer is the surveyor, marking the lines of future homesteads. Hard behind him are father, mother, boys and girls, to whom the nation gives this homestead thus designated. If the man is sick the woman nurses him. The children grow up to know the world they live in. The boundary of the nation is not a mere chain of garrisons nor the scattered posts of missions; it is a line of homes, founded with all that the word home involves.

All these lessons of three centuries point one way. They show that the world is not very good for wandering Apaches or Digger Indians, freezing and starving under hard winters when harvests have failed. To their point of view it was a world hard and cruel. To Franciscan friars, ruling a little empire which yielded none but physical harvests, where the garden, and orchard, and vineyard were only so many specks in the midst of an unbounded desert, the world can not have seemed a better world—a world made for wild horses, and further East for wild buffaloes, but not for men —"the great American Desert." It is not till man asserts the courage and freedom of a son of God, it is not till man appears with wife and child and proposes to establish his heaven here; it is not till then that he masters nature, and she gladly obeys him. Nay, then he has no success unless he appears as the vicegerent of God Himself, and establishes over this vast domain the empire of law, and speaks as God might speak, with "Thou shalt do this," and "Thou shalt not do that" in this empire.

The Old-World writers are fond of telling us that we owe the prosperity of this nation to its physical resources. It is not so. The physical resources have existed for centuries. It is only in the moral force of sons and daughters of God; it is such working power as takes the names of law, courage, independence, and family affection; it is only in these that our victory is won. The drunken swaggerer of the advance only checks the triumph. The miser, who would carry off his silver to use elsewhere, only hinders the advance. The victory comes from the hand of God to the children of God, who establish His empire in the magic spell of three great names. As always these names are: Faith, which gives courage; Hope, which determines to succeed; and Love, which builds up homes.

It is impossible to see the steps of such a victory without owning the infinite Power behind it all. You cannot use magnetic ore and coal for its smelting and the silicates for its fusion, all flung in together side by side, without asking if the Power who threw these price-

less gifts together where each was needed for
each did not know what He was doing. But
the buffalo passes over it, and the gopher
mines under it, and it might be so much gravel
of the sea. Savages pass over it, with no future, no heaven, and one would say no God.
It is worthless desert still, but one day a man
comes who deserves his name. He is a child
of God. He is determined that to-morrow
shall be better than to-day. He knows he is
lord of nature, and he bids her serve him.
The coal burns, the iron melts, the silicate
fuses. It is impossible to see that miracle and
not feel that for this man the world was
created, and for this world this man was born.
He is in his place. He did not have to seek it;
it was made for him. With him it is a garden.
Without him it is a desert. He can hew down
these mountains. He can fill up these valleys.
And where he has filled, and where he has
hewed, lo, the present heaven of happy homes!
It is thus that prophecy accomplishes itself,
and

"The car of the Lord rolls gloriously on."

MAGEE

THE MIRACULOUS STILLING OF THE STORM

BIOGRAPHICAL NOTE

WILLIAM CONNOR MAGEE, Archbishop of York, was born at Cork in 1821. Educated at Trinity College, Dublin, he was ordained in 1844. His first important charge was the Octagon Chapel at Bath in 1850. In 1864 he was made dean of Cork, and in 1868, Bishop of Peterborough. In 1891 he was appointed to succeed Dr. William Thomson, as Archbishop of York.

Dr. Magee was pronounced by Canon Liddon the greatest preacher of his day. His speech in the House of Lords in 1869 against Irish Disestablishment was said by the highest authorities, as quoted by Lord Salisbury, to be the finest speech ever delivered, in either house of Parliament, by any man then living. His oratory was characterized by clearness and terseness of expression, while his full-toned voice was capable of sounding every gradation of feeling. He died in 1891, three months after his enthronization in York Minster.

MAGEE

1821—1891

THE MIRACULOUS STILLING OF THE STORM

Lord save us: we perish. . . . Then he arose, and rebuked the winds and the sea; and there was a great calm.—Matt. viii., 25, 26.

THE story of this miracle reveals to us Christ entering into peril together with His Church. It records for us her faith and her prayer. It reveals to us His presence and His power. That faith has been her faith, that prayer has been her prayer, from that hour until now. In all the long perilous voyage of the Church from that hour, never has she unlearned yet her first prayer; never has she become entirely unconscious of her Lord. Sometimes with a great and a fearless faith that defied the most terrible tempests, sometimes with a little and a timid faith, that shrank from the first ripple upon the deep, but ever with her real faith have Christ's Church and Christ's disciples turned in the hour of their tribulation to seek their Lord. And never has that prayer been said in vain. Never from the Church at large, or from the solitary disciple in his terror, has that prayer gone up without an answer.

Never has the eye of faith sought, and sought in vain, the Savior. Ever has the praying Church or the praying disciple found the still present Christ; and we believe that it is so now. We believe that Christ our Lord is here in the midst of us now, and that our eye of faith may see Him, and our prayer of faith may reach Him. And if this be so now—if Christ's presence be a real fact amongst us now, and our prayer have really a might to reveal that presence—then, above all things, it concerns us, that we understand the nature of that prayer, and the manner of that presence, that we understand what it is we mean, and what will come of it when we say: "Lord, save us, or we perish."

We ask you, then, to-night, brethren, to consider these two things: the meaning of the Church's prayer; the manner of her Lord's presence. Now, when we use these words: "Lord, save: we perish," we are really rehearsing two articles of our belief. We are declaring, first of all, that we believe there is a Lord —that in the visible world there is an invisible God with His overruling, and controlling, and appointing will; and, in the next place, we believe that this God is our Lord Jesus Christ. In the first of these, we Christians agree with every religion that ever has been. In the second, we differ from all other religions. When we say that above nature there is a will and a personality, we say what every religion says. Religion is nothing else than the belief in the supernatural, in something above nature, in a person, in a will; and prayer is nothing but the speech of our spirit to that will, and the submission of our will to it. Prayer is the effort of the spirit of man to rise above the visible up to the region of the invisible and the personal, there to speak out his care or his need. There can, therefore, be no prayer without this element of religion; and there can be no religion without this fact of prayer. Without it, you have philosophy, you may have sentiment; but you cannot have a real, practical, every-day religion. And, therefore, all religions have believed in a God or gods, a Lord or lords. Turk, Jew, heathen, in like case, would have said to some lord or other: "Save, or we perish." But the Christian believes something more. He believes that his Lord has come down amongst men; that He has taken to Him human flesh, and lived a human life, and died, and risen again, for his salvation. He worships not only a lord, but the incarnate Lord; and so the Church speaks her twofold faith in her great hymn from the first to Christ as God: "We praise Thee, O God; we acknowledge Thee to be the Lord"—Thee, and none other, to be the God, and Thee to be the Lord, and Ruler, and Master of all things. You see, then, that there is something different in Christian prayer from all other prayer and worship, and that the difference consists in this: that it is distinctively and avowedly the prayer to an incarnate Christ.

Now, if there be this difference between this prayer and all other prayer, then there must be a corresponding difference in the feelings and in the practical results of such a religion; and I am about to ask you now to follow me while I endeavor to trace for you this difference between Christian prayer and all other prayer. It seems as if the story in the gospel of this miracle exactly sets out this difference—exactly shows us the distinctive nature of Christian prayer. The story, you observe, divides itself, naturally, into three parts. There is, first of all, the voyage before the storm; there is, then, the storm; and there is, then, the miraculous stilling of the storm. Now, you observe that in each of these three parts, we have one thing in common. We have man, in some way or other, encountering, or encountered by, the outward and visible world. The third of these—the stilling of the storm—differs from the other two in this, that it is miraculous and supernatural. Now, let us, for a moment, leave out this third part. There are some, you know, who say, that we should always leave it out, and be better without it. Let us leave out, then, this third or miraculous part of the story; and let us contrast the first and the second parts. And what have we got? We have got a most re-

markable contrast between the two scenes.
What is it we see in the first scene? We see
a man subduing nature. It was by the knowledge of the elements and the laws of nature,
that man learned thus to sail upon the deep;
and in that one fact you have represented for
you the whole of the material progress of
humanity—all the triumphs of science, all the
glory and the beauty of art, all that marvelous
mastery that man obtains by his inventive and
creative will over the secret powers of nature,
as he unlocks them one by one, and compels
her to tell him her deepest mysteries—all that
man has done as he has advanced from horizon to horizon of discovery, finding still new
worlds to conquer, until we stand amazed at
our own progress and the infinity of it, and
we say of man: "What manner of being is
this, that even the winds and the sea obey
him?" Yes, there is the man the lord of
nature. There is nothing supernatural there.
All is natural, all is orderly. Man is lord and
master. Nature is man's servant; and, therefore, there seems no room, there seems no
need for prayer. There is nothing, seemingly,
there to be had for the asking; there is everything, seemingly, there to be had for working.
Man is to be seen walking in the garden of
his own planting and his own fencing; and
he reaches out hands to unforbidden fruits of
knowledge; and he believes that at last he
shall gather even of the tree of life. He is a

god unto himself, and he sees no need for prayer.

And now we turn to the second scene, and what have we there? We have the direct contrast with this scene. We have there, not man subduing nature, but nature subduing man. We have the storm in which the elements are man's masters and not his servants; and he that one minute before was the boasting lord of nature is its toy and its sport. The very foam upon the crest of those billows is not more helpless in the grasp of the elements than the lord and the king of them; and they toss him to and fro, as the wind drives the stubble in the autumn. This is the terrible aspect of nature. This is nature in her might, and in her majesty, and in her pitilessness, and in her capriciousness—when nature seems everything, and man, in her awful presence, dwindles and dwarfs into very nothingness —when man, in the presence of the vastness of her solitude, and the might of her storms, and the terror of her earthquakes, seems no more before her, with his little cares and his sorrows, than the wee bubbles upon the head of the cataract. This is nature as she masters man. Is it, then, any wonder that, in the early struggles of mankind with this terrible visible power of the creature, men came to worship the creature—that they ascribed to every one of these powers a divinity, that in the voice of the wind, and in the roar of the sea, and in the raging of the fire, they saw the signs of a divine presence, and they said to these elements: "Spare us," or "Save us, or else we perish"? And so all creation became peopled with gods—cruel gods, capricious gods, vengeful gods, gods whom men bribed with blood, gods whom, even while they bribed them, they could not love, and did not believe that they loved them. This is the first and most terrible form of creature worship; this was the idolatry of the heathen. But mark this, that such a worship as this could not continue forever, could not continue long, because it is the worship of ignorance; it is the belief in the supernatural, only because it confuses the unknown with the supernatural. Ever as science advances must this faith melt away. Ever must the domain of the known push itself forward into the domain of the unknown. Ever does the man of science take one by one the gods of the man of superstition and break them upon their pedestals, and tell him this: "What you worship is no god. What you worship is no lord. It is not your lord. It is a servant of yours; and I class it in this or that rank of your servants." So, one by one, like ghosts and fantoms in the dawning of the day—one by one, the fantoms of gods that haunted the night of the old world vanish before the dawn of knowledge. But then it is a terrible daylight that breaks on men—a blank, dreary world in which men have no sight of the invisible, no sense of the supernatural. It is that last and most terrible aspect of nature, when she appears, not as many gods, or many wills, but as the great soulless piece of mechanism, of which we are only part—a terrible machinery in which we are, somehow or other, involved, and in the presence of which the sense of our free-will leaves us. The pith, and the manhood, and the vigor of men, and the beauty and the freedom of their life die out of them as they stand appalled before this passionless, this terrible, this awful face of a soulless world. This is the last and the most terrible form of creature worship. And mark this, that between these two aspects of nature, if you have no assured faith, there is no logical resting-place. Without the act of faith, you must take your choice between the superstition of ignorance or the atheism of knowledge.

And now we have seen these, we turn to the third portion of our story; and what is that we see there? We see, again, in this world of men, the miraculous and the supernatural. We hear a prayer, and we see a miracle. In the face of the might of nature and the terrors of her elements there arises up a Man in answer to man's cry—there is heard a Man's voice, which is yet the voice of God; and it rebukes the winds and the sea, and the elements of nature own their real Lord; and immediately there is a great calm. What is it, then, that we see? We see a miracle, and a miracle that answers to prayer; we see the living spirits of living men, in the hour of their agony and their distress, appealing from nature to the God of nature; and we have recorded the answer of God to man's prayer. The answer is, that God is Lord both of man and of nature; and we say, therefore, that the miracle, and the miracle alone, sufficiently justifies the prayer. We say that the reason why men may pray is, and can only be, that they know and believe, that there is a will which rules the visible. If you have not this belief, then believe us that all prayer, whatever men may say about it, is an unreality and a miserable mockery. To what am I to pray if I see no living God to pray to? Am I to pray to a law? Am I to pray to a system? Am I to pray to the winds, or to the waves, as men prayed of old? Am I to pray for physical blessings and deliverances? Men tell us we are not to pray, or to give thanks, concerning the rain or fruitful seasons, for that science has told us that the supernatural has no place there. Am I to pray then (for men do tell me that I may pray) only for spiritual and for moral gifts? Am I to pray only to be made wise, and good, and pure, and true, and holy? Ah! science is beginning to meet us there, too; for she is telling us, and telling us loudly, and telling us shamelessly, that here, too, there is no room, so far as she can tell, for prayer, as our mind is but a part of our body, and that our spiritual condition is a necessary result of our past history and of our present temperament—that we are what we are by virtue of birth and education, and country, and clime, and other things over which we have no control. And so the very spirit of man, all that is left of the invisible, vanishes before the approach of science. The knife of the anatomist lays bare, as he tells you, the secrets of man's being; and he finds no soul—he finds only the gray matter of the brain and the white threads of the nerves; and this is all that is left. Then, if we are not to pray, may we at least praise? Men say that if it is a folly to pray, at least it is a wisdom to praise; and they tell us this is the sentimental theory of the modern gospel. They tell you: "You may not pray,—prayer has no place in our system,—but you may praise; you may lift up your heart in hymns of joy and gratitude to the great Father of your being; you may have festival and flower-crowned processions in honor of the Supreme Being; yes, you may in fine weather, when you are sailing over summer seas, and the pleasant summer wind is filling the sails of your bark, and is wafting sweet odors from the flower-crowned shores along which youth, and hope, and joy are passing—then you may lift up your hearts in thanks to the Father that gave all these, if

you do not forget it. But how is it in foul
weather? How is it when the sky above us
darkens, and the white crests of the waves
beneath us are swelling sharp and fierce, and
the jagged edges of the rocks are projecting
for our shipwreck, and the wild waste of the
waters is yawning below us, and we tremble
and shudder at their depths, and the wild
wind blows our prayer back into our bosoms
—is that the time to sing sentimental hymns
to our great supreme Father and Giver of all
good? It is a time (thank God, thank Christ,
for this) when the Christian, when the disciple of Christ, may hold fast his faith and
say, "Tho he slay me, yet will I trust in him";
but it is not a time when the deist has breath
to sing his hymns to the supreme Author of
his being. No, we believe that there is a miracle that justifies, and alone justifies prayer.
We know that there are those (and they are
good and wise men, many of them) who con-
trive nice adjustments and philosophical ex-
planations how prayer may be reconciled with
universal law. We do not greatly care for
these. They may be right; they may be
wrong. In some future state and higher condition of our being we may know how far
they are true, how far they are false; but,
meanwhile, we need not be too nervously
anxious to make room for almighty God to
work His own will in His own world. We
believe in the miracle of creation; we believe

that there was once a voice that said, "Let
there be light, and there was light"; we believe that at the sound of that voice the universe leapt into life; and we believe in the
miracle of the Incarnation, when God took
human flesh and dwelt amongst men; we believe in the miracle of the descent of the
Spirit of God, when, with the miraculous
sound of the rushing wind and the miraculous
gleam of the fire, God once more came down
to dwell amongst men; we believe in the miracles that are written for us in this Book,
were they ten times as many as they are; we
believe that the sea has stood on one side like
a wall, and that the waters have gushed forth
from the rock; we believe that bread has been
rained from heaven; we believe that a touch
has awakened the dead—we believe all this;
and, because we believe it, we believe the voice
when it says to us, "Pray"; and because we
hear that voice still amongst us, and because
we know it to be the same voice, we say, as
we hear it, "Lord, save, or we perish."

But still, in the last place, it may be
said to us: If you do believe that there
is this power of miracle amongst you still,
and that it will answer to your prayer,
why is it that we do not see more miracles
than we do? Why is not the world filled
with strange miracles every day, consider-
ing the infinite number of men's needs, and
the infinite number of human prayers? My

brethren, it does seem to me that if we
were merely deists, and did not believe in
Christ, it would be difficult for us to answer
this objection. The spirit of man has, however (thanks be to God for it), in all ages been
deeper and truer in its instincts than his mere
logical power. Even the deist (and we thank-
fully acknowledge it), tho inconsistently and
illogically, yet really and truly prays. For
us Christians there is not any difficulty.
There is that difference in our prayer of
which I spoke. To whom is it that we pray?
Not merely to the invisible Lord or Creator
of the past, but to the incarnate Lord of the
present. We believe that Christ our Lord,
to whom we pray, took flesh and dwelt
amongst us, and we believe that He did so
that He might work the greatest of all miracles—the salvation of the souls of men; and
we believe that He wrought it by dying and
by living again. We believe that He established in the world this great and miraculous
law, that it is possible out of death to bring
life—nay, that death is the way to life. If
this be so, that by His death life was pur-
chased for us, then He teaches us that there
is another life than this, and that there is
another death and a deeper death than that
we fear; and He tells us, it may be, that even
by dying we shall be saved, that He will not
always save us from death—nay, that He may
save us by death. And so it comes to pass

that we understand how, by losing life, we may miraculously save it; and yet, on the other hand, by trying to save life, we may naturally lose it. So we come to understand this fact, how the beginning of His kingdom was full of miracles, and how, in the history of His kingdom, miracles have since ceased. The kingdom began with miracles that He might teach us that He was able to save; the miracles ceased in order that He might work a greater miracle. The lesser miracle of ruling nature ceased in order that the greatest of all miracles might perpetually be wrought —the regeneration, the redemption, and the glorification of the nature of man. And so we understand that Christ our Lord, because He is our Lord, may save us, even while we seem to perish, and to perish in His presence. He saved us of old by His agony and bloody sweat, by His cross and passion; and He will save us now, and He does save every child of His. Through agony and sweating, through cross and passion—through the agony of our long nights of spiritual darkness, through the sweat of long days of sore trouble and labor, beneath the weight of sharp and heavy crosses and sorrow, and through the bitterness of spiritual or bodily passion, does Christ our Lord still save those who cry to Him, even while He seems to sleep and not to hear them, as, in the bitterness of their souls, thinking themselves Christ-forsaken, they cry,

"Our Christ, our Christ, why hast Thou forsaken us? Dost Thou sleep, Lord? Save us, or we perish." And so you understand the peculiarity, the blest and the glorious peculiarity, of our Christian prayer. You understand the meaning of those deep words of Scripture—patience and the faith of the saints. You understand how the Christian man may pray and wait, and wait and pray still. If prayer were always followed by a miraculous answer, then prayer would be easy enough; or, on the other hand, if there were no thought of an answer, then it might be possible, tho not easy, to submit ourselves to the inevitable. But to pray and not to receive an answer, and yet to believe that the very not receiving is an answer; to cry, "Save, or we perish," and to seem about to perish; to believe that in what seems perishing is really salvation; to look for the living and watchful Christ, and to see what seems only the living and regardless Christ, and yet to believe that the time will come when, at His word, there shall be a great calm—this is the patience, this is the faith of those who worship an incarnate Lord. And so we trace the history of Christ's Church, and so we strive to trace the history of our own lives. Comparatively easy it is to trace the Church's history along her voyage. The Church gives time for comparing events and testing faith; and so, believing still in the presence of her

living Lord, the litanies of His Church ring
out, as they have ever rung, clearly and
loudly, and high above the roar of the tempest
and the rushing of the waters, still the prayer
is heard, "Good Lord, deliver us"; and still,
again and again, as the storm sweeps by, and
the Church passes out into calmer waters,
still comes the voice of thanksgiving: "He
hath delivered us." Even in our shorter
voyage, are there none of us who can remember times when we have knelt in agony and
wrestled in prayer with the Savior, who
seemed to have forgotten us, when the mighty
storm of temptation and the billows of calamity seemed about to destroy us, and when we
have cried (oh, how men do cry in those
storms of the soul, in those tempests and terrors of the heart, "Lord, save us, or we perish!" to Him to save us, and He has seemed
to sleep and to refuse to save? But at the last
we can remember how He did reveal Himself,
not stilling the raging storm when we would
have had Him still the terrible tempest, not
sparing, it may be, the precious bark that we
had rigged, and manned, and launched ourselves with trembling hopes and loving prayers, and watched with eyes tearless with
agony, as we saw it about to sink before us;
and we have been led to see and believe that
the living and the loving Lord was answering
even then our prayer, for the bark has, at
length, entered that haven where we would

be, and where the vexed waters of our voyage never awake a ripple on the calm depths of its eternal peace. This has been the experience of more than one of this great multitude that I see. And there is another experience that each one of you may have: it is when, in the troubles of your own spirit, when in the agonies of your own grief-stricken heart, when in the depths of your own repentance, when in the storms of your own fear and your own doubt, you cry to Christ the Savior—when you bring your sins as some men bring their sorrows, as anxious to have them removed as the others—when you cry to Christ your Savior: "Lord, save me! Save me, a sinner! Save me, an unprayerful man hitherto! Save me, an unbelieving man hitherto! Save me, not merely from the hell hereafter, but the present storm and depth of my own sins that threaten to destroy me! Save me, or I perish!" For, brethren, be sure of this, sooner or later this will be the experience of every such vexed and terrified soul—that, after he shall have endured, so long as his Lord sees good, the terrifying storm and the threatening deep that drive him in closer and closer search and seeking after his Lord, then, at last, there will appear the form of the Son of man, the form of Him who hung upon the cross, that He might for ever in the world's history work this great and, to Him, dearest of all miracles; and, at last, He will rebuke the winds and

37

the waves in that troubled soul, and there will be a great calm—a calm that may not last for ever, a calm that will not last for ever, for we have not yet reached the haven of perfect rest, but a calm that is a foretaste of the eternal rest. And so, praying with all our hearts to Christ our Lord, setting our will in submission to His will, pouring out our spirit in prayer to His Spirit, laying bare our hearts before His pure and loving eyes, through calm and through storm, praying still that we suffer not death in either, that we neither rot in the calm nor founder in the storm, praying still for His presence, praying still for grace to realize that presence, crying still for that deeper and yet deeper faith which is the result of more and more constant experience, crying still, "Lord, save, or we perish," wait in patience and in faith until He shall send His last messenger in this world, His angel of death, and bid him for us and in His name rebuke for the last time the winds that have vexed us, and the waves that have terrified us, and then with Him for ever there shall be a great calm.

SEISS

THE WONDERFUL TESTIMONIES

BIOGRAPHICAL NOTE

JOSEPH A. SEISS, Lutheran divine, was born in 1823, at Graceham, Md. He received his theological education as a private pupil of several clergymen and was first settled over churches at Martinsburg and Shepherdstown, Va. In 1843 he was transferred to Cumberland, then to Baltimore, Md., and finally became pastor of St. John's Church, Philadelphia, and for twelve years was editor of "The Lutheran." He died in 1904.

SEISS

1823—1904

THE WONDERFUL TESTIMONIES[1]

Thy testimonies are wonderful.—Psalms, cxix., 129.

THE Psalmist here addresses himself to God. The testimonies of which he speaks are God's testimonies. As collected and arranged in one book, they are known to us as the Bible. For the contents of these holy oracles the royal singer expresses his admiration. He pronounces them "wonderful."

It was not an unworthy theme with which he was occupied at the time, neither was it an extravagant opinion which he uttered. It is impossible that there should be for man a more important subject than the communications made to him from his God. And if ever there was a marvelous thing submitted to human inspection, it is this book, the holy Bible. It lies before us like an ocean, boundless and unfathomable,—like a Himalayan mountain, whose summit no foot of man has trod, and whose foundation is in the undiscovered heart of the world. To make a full

[1] Reprinted by permission of the Literary Trustees of the Dr. Seiss' Estate.

41

survey of it is not possible in the present condition of the human faculties. Even the inspired Paul, when he came to look into it,
found himself gazing into profundities at
which he could do no more than exclaim, "Oh,
the depth of the riches both of the wisdom
and the knowledge of God!" And yet there
are many beautiful shells and pebbles lying
on the shore of this sea, and as many precious
flowers blooming on this mountain side, which
any one may gather, and which, whosoever
attentively contemplates, must feel himself
impelled to join the admiring exclamation,
"The testimonies of the Lord are wonderful."

Let us look briefly at a few particulars by
which to verify this declaration, praying that
God may open our eyes to behold wondrous
things out of His law.

I. The testimonies of the Lord are wonderful in age and preservation.

The Bible is the oldest of books. Some portions of it are much more recent than others,
but a large part of it has come down from the
remotest antiquity and antedates all other
writings in the world. It contains a journal
of events which transpired centuries before
the building of the Pyramids. The book of
Job existed before Cadmus carried letters into
Greece. The five books of Moses were read
in holy assemblies two hundred years before
Sanchoniathon wrote. David and Solomon
had uttered their sacred songs and prophecies

half a century before Homer enraptured the
Greeks with his verses or Lycurgus had given
laws to Lacedæmon. Dozens of the books of
Scripture were complete a hundred years before the first public library was founded at
Athens; and the last of the prophets had
ended his message before Socrates, Plato, and
Aristotle had propounded their philosophies.
When the elements of society were but forming in the womb of the far-distant past, the
Bible was there. When the foundations of
earth's present greatness were laid, it was
there. And when we go back to the very beginnings of history, even there does its hand
lead us and its right hand uphold us.

Nor is it as a mere lifeless fossil that this
book has come down to us from such remote
antiquity. Tho hoary with age, its youthful
vigor remains, and its natural force is not
abated. It has only grown fresher with age,
and strengthened with every new trial. It
has been at the births and deaths of a hundred
mighty nations, and seen empires rise, flour-
ish, and fall, and coexisted with the longest
lines of earthly kings, and beheld some of the
sublimest monuments of human effort come
forth and disappear, and passed a hundred
generations in reaching us; but, withal, it still
lives, in all nations, in all languages, the most
precious legacy of departed ages, and the only
thing that remains to us from some of them.
Tho it has encountered many a fierce con-

43

flict with the hate of men and the spite of devils,—tho the object of many a concerted scheme to blot it from the earth,—tho often held up to ridicule, with "gigantic apes like Voltaire chattering at it, men of genius turned by some Circean spell into swine, like Mirabeau and Paine, casting filth at it, demoniacs whom it had half rescued and half inspired, like Rousseau, making mouths in its face,"and all the varied passions of unsanctified men continually arrayed against it,—it still holds its place as the most uncorrupt and authentic of histories, the most august and controlling of records, the most universal, venerable, and potent of books, imagining in its very history the stupendous majesty of the God whom it reveals.

II. The testimonies of the Lord are wonderful in their authorship.

They are not of man, but of God. We can not now refer to the varied and multitudinous considerations which enter into the proofs of this. It is capable, however, of being established by the very highest moral evidences. The wisest and best men of every age have concurred in receiving the Scriptures as from God. And it is not possible to give a rational account of their origin, and the source of their contents, without ascribing them to the divine authorship which they claim.

It may seem strange that the infinite God should condescend to put His great thoughts into the poor language of mortals, to communicate with creatures so dull and stupid as the sons of men; but this He has done. Portions of the Scriptures are made up of the very words of God, articulated by Himself in the hearing of men commissioned to declare them. One chapter, which embodies the moral essence of all the rest, was engraven by His own finger upon tables of rock, and delivered to Moses all ready formed and set in the alphabetic signs employed by men. Other parts consist of communications of celestial messengers sent directly from heaven's throne to declare God's will and purposes to the dwellers upon earth. A still larger portion was taken down as it fell from the lips of One in whom God had incarnated Himself, and whose every word and act in this world was a revelation from the unknown Deity. Even those parts which were written by men were produced by mysterious motion and illumination of the Holy Ghost,—by inspiration of God. Indeed, the whole book is a literary aerolite, all the characteristics of which are unearthly, and whose own superior attributes are so many demonstrations of its superhuman source. Its very address is so far above that of man, that no mortal, unprompted, could ever have risen to it. Its subjects are all treated after an unearthly manner. Every leaf of it bears the sunlight of some higher sphere. Every page has on it the imprimatur of God. And all its words are instinct with divine fires, flashing the admonition upon every reader, "Put off thy shoes from off thy feet, for the place whereon thou standest is holy ground." They that look upon it look upon expressions of the eternal Spirit. They that rightly take its lessons drink in living emanations from unsearchable Godhead. It is the abiding miracle of *rapport* with the Mind which projected, upholds, and governs the universe. It is the Word of God.

III. The testimonies of the Lord are wonderful in their originality and instructiveness.

The Bible depends upon no discoveries of man, and leans upon no other books. If it says some things which may be learned elsewhere, its utterances are always independent and peculiarly its own. The world through which it ranges is much wider than that of man's thoughts. It goes back to a remoter antiquity; it takes in a broader space; it extends to a vaster future; it introduces to sublimer spheres and forms of being; and it exhibits a much profounder wisdom. It opens arcana of which no earthly powers ever dreamed, and is at home in regions where the sublimest imaginings of man had hardly extended a guess. On all the great questions of theology, life, death, and futurity, it speaks with a familiarity, comprehensiveness, and propriety which at once command our con-

fidence and satisfy our hearts. What it
touches, it touches with a master's hand. It
never speaks without pregnant meaning in
all its words. And there is nothing in human
science, poetry, or tradition which it does not
exceed in knowledge, wisdom, and real value.

In its account of the creation, and the origin
of things, there is nothing to compare with
it. In all the historians, philosophers, and
secular authors,—the books of Zoroaster, the
records of Phœnicia and Egypt, the Dialogues
of Plato and Lucian, the annals of China,
the treatises of Plutarch, the Shastras of
India, the Edda of Scandinavia, and all the
schemes that have ever been given in explanation of the earth's primal history,—there is
nothing so natural, so magnificent, so simple,
so appropriate, so reliable, so satisfactory, as
the first chapter of Genesis. Nor have all the
discoveries of modern geology brought forward anything to convict Moses of a false
cosmogony. If it is a truth that the history
of the earth's formation runs back through
uncounted ages, he leaves an interval for it,
between "the beginning" and the period
when God caused light to appear upon its
dark and misty surface. If it is true that
vast eras have been traversed by each separate
order of living things, one after the other, we
find precisely the same succession in the
Mosaic account which is found preserved in
the different layers of the earth's crust. And

47

if it be true that there was life upon our world ages and cycles of ages before the period noted in Genesis as that in which man was created, it is also true that no traces of human existence are found except in the most recent deposits. A certain stonemason of the village of Cromartie, with sledge and chisel, himself delved through every formation, from the surface-mold down through the old red sandstone to the Silurian, gneiss, and granite, and, having mastered all that is known concerning each, has written it down as the result of his marvelous explorations, that the truthfulness of the Mosaic record is engraven upon the rocks forever.

And so in every department of science the Bible is always true to nature, and has invariably been in advance of all human investigations and discoveries. How many thousands of years have metaphysicians and psychologists been at work to map out, classify, and gauge the various capacities and powers of the human mind and soul! But they have found no way of approach to the heart so masterly and effective as that taken by the Scriptures; and the more that is known of the nature of the man, the more clearly is it seen that the Bible comprehended it from the commencement. It has been but a few years since Newton laid open the laws of gravitation; and yet the Scriptures spoke of the earth being hung "upon nothing," as if familiar

with the whole subject, before human science
had begun to form even its feeblest guesses in
the case. It has only been since the invention
of the telescope enabled men to search through
the starry spaces that Sir John Herschel has
discovered in the northern sky a peculiar bar-
renness; but more than three thousand years
ago Job told Bildad the Shuhite that "God
stretched out the north over the empty place."
It has been but a few years since science discovered "that the sun is not the dead center
of motion, around which comets sweep and
planets whirl," but that "the earth and sun,
with their splendid retinue of comets, satel-
lites, and planets, are all in motion around
some point or center of attraction inconceiv-
ably remote, and that that point is in the direction of the star Alcyone, one of the Pleiades"; which would hence seem to be "the
midnight throne" in which the whole system
of gravitation has its central seat and from
which all material orbs are governed. But
the Bible asked the question, more than thirty
centuries ago, "Canst thou bind the sweet influences of Pleiades?" as if the speaker knew
all about the facts in the case. How long has
it been since the doctrine of the rotundity of
the earth has been settled by scientific men?
yet the Psalmist spoke of "the round world";
and Solomon described in brief the true theory
of wind-currents, and strongly hinted the cir-
culation of the blood, at least twenty-five

hundred years ago. And, with all the advances of knowledge which have so wonderfully marked the last three hundred years, in which the spirit of philosophic inquiry has ranged the universe, searched heaven, earth, and sea, knocked at every door, peered into every recess, consulted every oracle of nature, and gathered trophies of power and treasures of wisdom and sublimities of knowledge at which the world has been amazed,—in all the motions which the experimentist has traced, in all the principles of power which the master of physics has discovered, in all the combinations which the chemist has detected, in all the forms which the naturalist has recorded, in all the spiritual phenomena which the metaphysician has described, and in all the conditions and relations of mind or matter, past or present, which human research has found out,—there has not come to light one truth to contradict these holy records, or to require the relinquishment or change of one word in all the great volume of Scripture.

IV. The testimonies of the Lord are wonderful in beauty and literary excellence.

The Bible is a casket of jewelry of the richest hues and the most exquisite workmanship. Sir William Jones, that great Orientalist and scholar, has said, "I have regularly and attentively perused these Holy Scriptures, and am of the opinion that this volume, independently of its divine origin, contains more true sublimity, more exquisite beauty, more pure morality, more important history, and finer strains of poetry and eloquence, than can be collected from all other books, in whatever age or language they may have been written." Even Rousseau wrote, "The majesty of the Scriptures strikes me with admiration. The works of our philosophers, with all their pomp of diction, how mean, how contemptible, in comparison with them!"

Nor does it matter much what part of the Scriptures we take, or in what department of rhetoric we test them. Whether it be history or prophecy, the Old Testament or the New, narrative or description, poetry or prose, the same characteristics are to be seen. Moses is as pure and simple as Adam and Eve in Paradise, and yet as majestic and grand as that great creation which he describes. Job contains a drama which is without a parallel,—a drama of facts in which heaven and earth, visible and invisible, with all their wonderful interpenetrations, are set out in their connection with a suffering saint upon his couch, and in which the spirit of earnest inquiry urges itself fcrward until everything comes forth to declare the majesty of God, and all the might and goodness of man lies prostrate before Him who "bringeth forth Mazzaroth in his season" and speaketh comfortably to them that trust in Him. Under the leadership of David's muse, we pass

51

through varied scenes of beauty and grandeur,
—pastures and glens, still waters and roaring
floods, dismal swamps and silent wildernesses,
forests crashing with the lightnings of God
and tempests that convulse the seas, the smoke
and fury of battle and the shoutings of glad
multitudes, by dells of lonely sorrow and
along the starry archways of the sky,—until
at length we take our places in a temple high
as heaven and wide as space, with all objects
of creation as living worshipers around us,
each with its separate hymn of grateful joy,
blending in one almighty adoration. Isaiah
rises upon us like some "mighty orb of song,"
whose rays are streaming minstrelsies, that
have thrilled upon the hearts of men for seventy generations, and which must needs thrill
on, unrivaled in their kind, while earth and
time endure. Ezekiel is a very comet of fire,
flaming his impetuous way across the heavens,
and, like the living spirits in his own first
vision, going and returning as a flash of lightning. And throughout,—the Evangelists
with their simple story of Jesus, and Paul in
his epistles and orations, and John in his
loving letters and apocalyptic visions,—from
the first words, "In the beginning," onward
to the last "amen," we find variety, beauty,
pathos, dignity, sweetness, magnificence, and
glory, such as are contained in no other com-
position. Here are the sublimest heights and
the profoundest depths, and all the gradations

from the one to the other. From the worm that grovels in the dust, to the leviathan in the foaming deep, and the supreme archangel, and the eternal God; from the hyssop on the wall, to the cedars of Lebanon, and the healing trees which shade life's eternal river; from the pearl-drops which trickle from the mountain rock, to the noise of dashing torrents, and the wide waters of the deluge; from the glowworm under the thorn, to the sun in the heavens, and the great Father of Lights; from the lone pilgrim to the triumphing host, and the gathering multitude which no man can number; from the deepest sorrows of the lost, to the probation scenes of earth and the seraphic visions of the blest,—there is nothing known to mortals which God hath not brought into requisition to intensify and adorn the precious book which He has given to men. As an eloquent preacher beyond the sea remarks, "He has filled it with marvelous incident and engaging history, with sunny pictures from Old-World scenery and affecting anecdotes from patriarchal times. He has replenished it with stately argument and thrilling verse, and sprinkled it over with sententious wisdom and proverbial pungency. It has the gracefulness of high utility; it has the majesty of intrinsic power; it has the charm of its own sanctity: it never labors, never strives, but, instinct with great realities and bent on blessed ends, has all the translucent beauty and unstudied power which you might expect from its lofty object and all-wise Author.''

Some call these Scriptures dull and uninviting; but there is no book in being with so many real attractions. There is no classic equal to it,—no historian like Moses, no poet like Job or Isaiah, no singer like David, no orator like Paul, no character like Jesus, and no revelation of God or nature like that which these venerable pages give. Not without reason has Sir Thomas Browne said, ''Were it of man, I could not choose but say it was the singularest and superlative piece that hath been extant since the creation. Were I a pagan, I should not refrain the lecture of it, and can not but commend the judgment of Ptolemy, that thought not his library complete without it.''

V. The testimonies of the Lord are wonderful in their influences and effects.

The Bible has been, for three thousand years, one of the greatest potencies on earth. It has been, and is to this moment, a greater power than Rome, or Greece, or Babylon ever was. Though it has not conquered the world, it has advanced further towards it than Alexander ever did. It has done more to govern and renew the human heart than all the laws enacted by legislators, and all the maxims devised by uninspired sages, and all the lessons, apart from itself, that were ever given to the race. It is the chief stay of a society which for a thousand years has been the most widespread, the most important, and the most powerful association on the earth. It has controlled the religious opinions of a large part of mankind for nearly forty centuries. It has molded characters and directed the efforts of men whose lives and labors introduced new eras and shaped the destinies of nations and turned the course of the world's entire history. It has begotten and fostered the purest virtue, the sublimest manhood, the noblest beneficence, the sincerest charity, the tenderest kindness, and all the blessed saintship, that have ever been upon earth.

Its vast influence upon the welfare of nations may be estimated in part from the bloody codes, and infamous administrations, and social degradations, and far-reaching wretchedness, of those countries where it is rejected or unknown, contrasted with the blessedness and peace of those who have received it. It was the great Milton who said, "There are no politics like those which the Scriptures teach"; and in proof we need only look at Judea when it knew no laws but those which this book contains. How smooth and steady were the wheels of public justice, and how beautiful was the flow of national peace, in those golden days of the old Hebrew commonwealth! How did the joyous vines, and fields of waving ears, and gold of Ophir, and flocks and cattle abiding on a thousand hills, and cities full of peace and plenty, proclaim abroad the wealth and blessedness of that goodly land! How did the voice of singing and the fragrance of virtue linger round each habitation, and the sacrifices of praise crowd all the temple's courts from tribes rejoicing in the smiles of God!

In the sphere of learning and thought-creations, also, the influence of the Bible is equally marked and wonderful. It is to the world of letters what the sun is to the solar system, the fountain of the purest light and brightest wisdom. It has produced more books than any other one thing in existence. It has fostered learning when there was no other stimulation to its cultivation felt. Even the heathen classics owe their preservation to it. As a book written in other times, places, and languages, it has called forth the most laboriously compiled lexicons, grammars, and works on archeology by which the world of the present communes with the world of the past. As a book claiming the faith and obedience of men, it has created a world of learned apology, comment, and exposition, and some of the noblest specimens of argument, eloquence, and appeal which are known to man. And, simply as a book among books, it has wrought wondrously upon the thoughts and productions of authors of all classes. The Visions of Dante are largely drawn from it.

Every canto of the Faerie Queene bears the impress of its influence. Milton's matchless songs of Paradise are from an inspiration which the Bible alone could give. From the same source came the immortal dream of Bunyan, the Pauline reasonings of Barrow, the flaming zeal of Richard Baxter, the "molten wealth" and "lava of gold and gems" which poured down "the russet steep of Puritan theology," the songs of Cowper, and "Thoughts" of Young, and visions of Pollok, and mighty eloquence of the Luthers, the Knoxes, the Massillons, the Whitefields, and the Halls. Addison, and Thomson, and Burke, and Dryden, and Wordsworth, and Coleridge, and Southey, and Campbell, and Goethe, all are vastly indebted to the Scriptures for whatever excellences are found in their works. Shakespeare drew largely from this same precious mine, and also even Hobbes, and Shelley, and Byron. That prince of modern orators, Daniel Webster, once said, "If there be anything in my style or thoughts to be commended, the credit is due to my kind parents in instilling into my mind an early love of the Scriptures." Indeed, if we were to destroy the Bible, and take from the world of literature and thought all that it has contributed directly or indirectly, half the history of the race would be swept out of mind, the noblest ideas that have swelled man's heart would be gone, some of the proudest

monuments of human genius would be buried
in oblivion, and thick darkness would settle
down upon the world forever.

VI. The testimonies of the Lord are wonderful as a fountain of consolation, hope and
salvation.

The Bible to all its other excellences adds
this, that it is the Book of Life. It is not
only a basket of silver network, but it contains
apples of gold. It is the record of glad tidings to a perishing world, a message of joy
to all people. In it, Wisdom hath mingled
her wine, and slain her fatlings, and furnished
her table, and calls all the hungry and needy
to come and partake. The entrance of its
words giveth light and imparteth understanding to the simple, and maketh wise unto salvation. It is a balm from Gilead for the sick,
oil for the bruises of the wounded, reprieve
for the prison-bound, and bread for them that
are ready to perish. Its different books are
but so many angels of mercy, carrying contentment into the abodes of poverty, enabling
even the children of want to lift up their
eyes to God who ordereth all things well, and
to eat their scanty meals in peace; staying the
hearts of the persecuted and opprest, causing them to rejoice and sing under the yoke,
at the stake, and in the hottest of the fires,
as on their passage-way to crowns immortal
in the world to come; calming the minds of
the fevered, mollifying where all earthly

medicines fail, and kindling glad hopes of recompense yet to be revealed; lighting up comforts in the breasts of those that mourn for their dead, and assuring them of blessed reunions in a better life; and kindling even the dying eye and inspiring the dying heart with thoughts of speedy triumph, causing lips already closed for death to open once more in utterances of victory.

We may talk of the venerable age of the Bible, and its scientific accuracy, and its literary beauty and sublimity, and its wonderful influences upon the ideas, laws, governments, and general order of society and mankind; but it is all nothing in comparison with the spiritual good and immortal hopes and consolations which it begets in those who receive it as a message from their God. Are we voyagers upon a troubled and a dangerous sea? Here is a chart by which to steer in safety to the happy shores. Are we soldiers, beset with foes and required to endure the shocks of battle? This is an armory from which all needed weapons may be drawn at will, and by the right use of which we may hew our way to immortal triumph. Are we pilgrims and strangers, worn and weary in our search for the home from which we are exiles? In this book gush out the pure, fresh waters of life, the cooling shades from the Rock of salvation appear, and the guiding word is heard from pilgrims in advance, to cheer and encourage us till we reach the mansion of our Father. Indeed, it is beyond the power of language to express the excellency and richness of spiritual treasure which we have in this holy Book. It is the miraculous cruse of the Shunamitess which never exhausts. It is the wand of Moses which swallows the serpents of life, and parts the sea of trouble, and brings forth waters in the thirsty wilderness. It is the ladder of Jacob on which our spirits ascend to commune with God and angels. It is the telescope of faith by which we look on things invisible, survey even the third heavens, and have present to our view what is to be in afterages. It is the chariot of Elijah in which to ride up the starry way to immortality unhurt of death. It is the channel of the almighty Spirit as it goes forth for the sanctification of the race,—the very gulf-stream of eternal life as it pours out for the resuscitation of our wilted and decaying world.

Allusion has been made to the dreadful eclipse it would be to the world of letters and thought, for the Bible, and what it has done for man, to be blotted out. But that were nothing to the moral and spiritual night that would go along with such a calamity. Besides carrying away with it a vast proportion of the intellectual and moral life of the last eighteen centuries, it would silence every preacher of salvation, and abolish at once his office and his text. It would stop every work of mercy and plan of philanthropy in the world.

It would transmute into a lie all our fond anticipations of the return of Jesus to renew the world, restore our dead, complete our salvation, and bring us to an eternal heaven. It would hush forever the glad tidings with which men have comforted themselves for these many weary ages. It would put out the mother's hopes of her dead babes, quench the wife's fond desires for her husband's everlasting peace, destroy the widow's consolation as she lingers by the grave of her buried love, and extinguish the matron's last comfort as she trembles on the verge of eternity.

It would take with it all the reliefs and blessedness which prayer in the name of Jesus gives, and leave the sinner without pardon in the extremities of life. It would take away the last appeal of the slave against his oppressor, remove the last check of tyranny, and lift from the wicked hearts of men the last restraints, giving carnival to every lust and play to every passion, without correction, without limit, and without end!

We stagger, and are horrified, at the mere idea of the loss that would be inflicted. Chills run down our pulses at the contemplation of the despair and wretchedness which would ensue.

Let us, then, learn to value the possession of such a precious book. Let us bind it to our hearts as our chief treasure in this sin-darkened world. And, whilst we admire its beauty and revere its mysteries, let us abide by its precepts, and, as far as in us lies, practise its sacred mandates.

MACLAREN

THE PATTERN OF SERVICE

BIOGRAPHICAL NOTE

ALEXANDER MACLAREN was born in 1826, educated at Glasgow University, for twelve years preached at Southampton, and afterwards for many years in Manchester. Besides an impressive face and figure he brought to the pulpit a ripe scholarship, an almost perfect English style, and an uncommonly vigorous personality. The keynote of his life and character is disclosed in his own words, uttered in Manchester:

"I have been so convinced that I was best serving all the varied social, economical, and political interests that are dear to me by preaching what I conceived to be the gospel of Jesus Christ, that I have limited myself to that work. I am sure, with a growing conviction day by day, that so we Christian ministers best serve our generation. My work, whatever yours may be, is, and has been for thirty-eight years, and I hope will be for a little while longer yet, to preach Jesus Christ as the King of England and the Lord of all our communities, and the Savior and friend of the individual soul."

MACLAREN

THE PATTERN OF SERVICE[1]

He touched his tongue; and looking up to heaven, He sighed, and saith, Ephphatha, that is, Be opened.—
Mark vii., 33, 34.

FOR what reason was there this unwonted slowness in Christ's healing works? For what reason was there this unusual emotion ere He spoke the word which cleansed?

As to the former question, a partial answer may perhaps be that our Lord is here on half-heathen ground, where aids to faith were much needed, and His power had to be veiled that it might be beheld. Hence the miracle is a process rather than an act; and, advancing as it does by distinct stages, is conformed in appearance to men's works of mercy, which have to adapt means to ends, and creep to their goal by persevering toil. As to the latter, we know not why the sight of this one poor sufferer should have struck so strongly on the ever-tremulous chords of Christ's pitying heart; but we do know that it was the vision

[1] From "The Secret of Power, and Other Sermons," published by Funk & Wagnalls Company.

brought before His spirit by this single instance of the world's griefs and sicknesses, in which mass, however, the special case before Him was by no means lost, that raised His eyes to heaven in mute appeal, and forced the groan from His breast.

The missionary spirit is but one aspect of the Christian spirit. We shall only strengthen the former as we invigorate the latter. Harm has been done, both to ourselves and to this great cause, by seeking to stimulate compassion and efforts for heathen lands by the use of other excitements, which have tended to vitiate even the emotions they have aroused, and are apt to fail us when we need them most. It may therefore be profitable if we turn to Christ's own manner of working, and His own emotions in His merciful deeds, set forth in this remarkable narrative, as containing lessons for us in our missionary and evangelistic work. I must necessarily omit more than a passing reference to the slow process of healing which this miracle exhibits. But that, too, has its teaching for us, who are so often tempted to think ourselves badly used, unless the fruit of our toil grows up, like Jonah's gourd, before our eyes. If our Lord was content to reach His end of blessing step by step, we may well accept patient continuance in well-doing as the condition indispensable to reaping in due season.

But there are other thoughts still more

needful which suggest themselves. Those minute details which this evangelist ever delights
to give of our Lord's gestures, words, looks,
and emotions, not only add graphic force to
the narrative, but are precious glimpses of the
very heart of Christ. That fixed gaze into
heaven, that groan which neither the glories
seen above nor the conscious power to heal
could stifle, that most gentle touch, as if re-
moving material obstacles from the deaf ears,
and moistening the stiff tongue that it might
move more freely in the parched mouth, that
word of authority which could not be want-
ing even when His working seemed likest a
servant's, do surely carry large lessons for
us. The condition of all service, the cost of
feeling at which our work must be done, the
need that the helpers should identify themselves with the sufferers, and the victorious
power of Christ's word over all deaf ears—
these are the thoughts which I desire to con-
nect with our text, and to commend to your
meditation to-day.

We have here set forth the foundation and
condition of all true work for God in the
Lord's heavenward look.

The profound questions which are involved
in the fact that, as man, Christ held communion with God in the exercise of faith and
aspiration, the same in kind as ours, do not
concern us here. I speak to those who believe
that Jesus is for us the perfect example of

complete manhood, and who therefore believe
that He is "the leader of faith," the head of
the long procession of those who in every age
have trusted in God and been lightened. But,
perhaps, tho that conviction holds its place
in our creeds, it has not been as completely
incorporated with our thoughts as it should
have been. There has, no doubt, been a tendency, operating in much of our evangelical
teaching, and in the common stream of ortho-
dox opinion, to except, half unconsciously, the
exercises of the religious life from the sphere
of Christ's example, and we need to be re-
minded that Scripture presents His vow, "I
will put my trust in Him," as the crowning
proof of His brotherhood, and that the prints
of His kneeling limbs have left their impres-
sions where we kneel before the throne. True,
the relation of the Son to the Father involves
more than communion—namely, unity. But
if we follow the teaching of the Bible, we shall
not presume that the latter excludes the former, but understand that the unity is the
foundation of perfect communion, and the
communion the manifestation, so far as it can
be manifested, of the unspeakable unity. The
solemn words which shine like stars—starlike
in that their height above us shrinks their
magnitude and dims their brightness, and in
that they are points of radiance partially dis-
closing, and separated by, abysses of unlighted
infinitude—tell us that in the order of eter-

nity, before creatures were, there was communion, for "the Word was with God," and there was unity, for "the Word was God." And in the records of the life manifested on earth the consciousness of unity loftily utters itself in the unfathomable declaration, "I and my Father are one"; whilst the consciousness of communion, dependent like ours on harmony of will and true obedience, breathes peacefully in the witness which He leaves to Himself: "The Father has not left me alone for I do always the things that please him."

We are fully warranted in supposing that that wistful gaze to heaven means, and may be taken to symbolize, our Lord's conscious direction of thought and spirit to God as He wrought His work of mercy. There are two distinctions to be noted between His communion with God and ours before we can apply the lesson to ourselves. His heavenward look was not the renewal of interrupted fellowship, but rather, as a man standing firmly on firm rock may yet lift his foot to plant it again where it was before, and settle himself in his attitude before he strikes with all his might; so we may say Christ fixes Himself where He always stood, and grasps anew the hand that He always held, before He does the deed of power. The communion that had never been broken was renewed; how much more the need that in our work for God the renewal of the —alas! too sadly sundered—fellowship should ever precede and always accompany our efforts! And again, Christ's fellowship was with the Father. Ours must be with the Father through the Son. The communion to which we are called is with Jesus Christ, in whom we find God.

The manner of that intercourse, and the various discipline of ourselves with a view to its perfecting, which Christian prudence prescribes, need not concern us here. As for the latter, let us not forget that a wholesome and wide-reaching self-denial cannot be dispensed with. Hands that are full of gilded toys and glass beads cannot grasp durable riches, and eyes that have been accustomed to glaring lights see only darkness when they look up to the violet heaven with all its stars. As to the former, every part of our nature above the simply animal is capable of God, and the communion ought to include our whole being.

Christ is truth for the understanding, authority for the will, love for the heart, certainty for the hope, fruition for all the desires, and for the conscience at once cleansing and law. Fellowship with Him is no indolent passiveness, nor the luxurious exercise of certain emotions, but the contact of the whole nature with its sole adequate object and rightful Lord.

Such intercourse, brethren, lies at the foundation of all work for God. It is the condition of all our power. It is the measure of all our success. Without it we may seem to realize the externals of prosperity, but it will be all illusion. With it we may perchance seem to spend our strength for naught; but heaven has its surprizes; and those who toiled, nor left their hold of their Lord in all their work, will have to say at last with wonder, as they see the results of their poor efforts, "Who hath begotten me these? behold, I was left alone; these, where had they been?"

Consider in few words the manifold ways in which the indispensable prerequisite of all right effort for Christ may be shown to be communion with Christ.

The heavenward look is the renewal of our own vision of the calm verities in which we trust, the recourse for ourselves to the realities which we desire that others should see. And what is equal in persuasive power to the simple utterance of your own intense conviction? He only will infuse his own religion into other minds, whose religion is not a set of hard dogmas, but is fused by the heat of personal experience into a river of living fire. It will flow then, not otherwise. The only claim which the hearts of men will listen to, in those who would win them to spiritual beliefs, is that ancient one: "That which we have seen with our eyes, which we have looked upon, declare we unto you." Mightier than all arguments, than all "proofs of the truth of the Christian religion," and penetrating

into a sphere deeper than that of the understanding, is the simple proclamation, "We
have found the Messias." If we would give
sight to the blind, we must ourselves be gazing into heaven. Only when we testify of
that which we see, as one might who, standing
in a beleaguered city, discerned on the horizon
the filmy dust-cloud through which the spear-
heads of the deliverers flashed at intervals,
shall we win any to gaze with us till they too
behold and know themselves set free.

Christ has set us the example. Let our
prayers ascend as His did, and in our measure
the answers which came to Him will not fail
us. For us, too, "praying, the heavens" shall
be "opened," and the peace-bringing spirit
fall dove-like on our meek hearts. For us,
too, when the shadow of our cross lies black
and gaunt upon our paths, and our souls are
troubled, communion with heaven will bring
the assurance, audible to our ears at least,
that God will glorify Himself even in us. If,
after many a weary day, we seek to hold fellowship with God as He sought it on the
Mount of Olives, or among the solitudes of
the midnight hills, or out in the morning
freshness of the silent wilderness, like Him
we shall have men gathering around us to
hear us speak when we come forth from the
secret place of the Most High. If our prayer,
like His, goes before our mighty deeds, the
voice that first pierced the skies will penetrate

the tomb, and make the dead stir in their grave-clothes. If our longing, trustful look is turned to the heavens, we shall not speak in vain on earth when we say, "Be opened."

Brethren, we cannot do without the communion which our Master needed. Do we delight in what strengthened Him? Does our work rest upon the basis of inward fellowship with God which underlay His? Alas! that our pattern should be our rebuke, and the readiest way to force home our faults on our consciences should be the contemplation of the life which we say that we try to copy!

We have here pity for the evils we would remove set forth by the Lord's sigh.

What was it that drew that sigh from the heart of Jesus? One poor man stood before Him, by no means the most sorely afflicted of the many wretched ones whom He healed. But He saw in him more than a solitary instance of physical infirmities. Did there not roll darkly before His thoughts that whole weltering sea of sorrow that moans round the world, of which here is but one drop that He could dry up? Did there not rise black and solid against the clear blue, to which He had been looking, the mass of man's sin, of which these bodily infirmities were but a poor symbol as well as a consequence? He saw as none but He could bear to see, the miserable realities of human life. His knowledge of all that man might be, of all that the most of men were becoming, His power of contemplating in one awful aggregate the entire sum of sorrows and sins, laid upon His heart a burden which none but He has ever endured. His communion with Heaven deepened the dark shadow on earth, and the eyes that looked up to God and saw Him could not but see foulness where others suspected none, and murderous messengers of hell walking in darkness unpenetrated by mortal sight. And all that pain of clearer knowledge of the sorrowfulness of sorrow, and the sinfulness of sin, was laid upon a heart in which was no selfishness to blunt the sharp edge of the pain nor any sin to stagnate the pity that flowed from the wound. To Jesus Christ, life was a daily martyrdom before death had "made the sacrifice complete," and He bore our griefs, and carried our sorrows through many a weary hour before He "bare them in his own body on the tree." Therefore, "Bear ye one another's burden, and so fulfil the law" which Christ obeyed, becomes a command for all who would draw men to Him. And true sorrow, a sharp and real sense of pain, becomes indispensable as preparation for, and accompaniment to, our work.

Mark how in us, as in our Lord, the sigh of compassion is connected with the look to heaven. It follows upon that gaze. The evils are more real, more terrible, by their startling contrast with the unshadowed light which

lives above cloudracks and mists. It is a sharp
shock to turn from the free sweep of the
heavens, starry and radiant, to the sights that
meet us in "this dim spot which men call
earth." Thus habitual communion with God
is the root of the truest and purest compassion. It does not withdraw us from our fellow feeling with our brethren, it cultivates no
isolation for undisturbed beholding of God.
It at once supplies a standard by which to
measure the greatness of man's godlessness,
and therefore of his gloom, and a motive for
laying the pain of these upon our hearts, as
if they were our own. He has looked into
the heavens to little purpose who has not
learned how bad and how sad the world now
is, and how God bends over it in pitying love.

And that same fellowship, which will clear
our eyes and soften our hearts, is also the one
consolation which we have when our sense of
all the ills that flesh is heir to becomes deep,
near to despair. When one thinks of the real
facts of human life, and tries to conceive of
the frightful meanness and passion and hate
and wretchedness, that has been howling and
shrieking and gibbering and groaning through
dreary millenniums, one's brain reels, and
hope seems to be absurdity, and joy a sin
against our fellows, as a feast would be in a
house next door to where was a funeral. I
do not wonder at settled sorrow falling upon
men of vivid imagination, keen moral sense,

and ordinary sensitiveness, when they brood
long on the world as it is. But I do wonder
at the superficial optimism which goes on with
its little prophecies about human progress,
and its rose-colored pictures of human life,
and sees nothing to strike it dumb for ever in
men's writhing miseries, blank failures, and
hopeless end. Ah! brethren, if it were not
for the heavenward look, how could we bear
the sight of earth! "We see not yet all things
put under him." No, God knows, far enough
off from that. Man's folly, man's submission
to the creatures he should rule, man's agonies,
and man's transgression, are a grim contrast
to the psalmist's vision. If we had only earth
to look to, despair of the race, exprest in settled melancholy apathy, or in fierce cynicism,
were the wisest attitude. But there is more
within our view than earth; "we see Jesus";
we look to the heaven, and as we behold the
true man, we see more than ever, indeed, how
far from that pattern we all are; but we can
bear the thought of what men as yet have
been, when we see that perfect example of
what men shall be. The root and the consolation of our sorrow for man's evils is communion with God.

We have here loving contact with those
whom we would help, set forth in the Lord's
touch.

The reasons for the variety observable in
Christ's method of communicating superna-

tural blessing were, probably, too closely connected with unrecorded differences in the spiritual conditions of the recipients to be distinctly traceable by us. But tho we cannot tell why a particular method was employed in a given case, why now a word, and now a symbolic action, now the touch of His hand, and now the hem of His garment, appeared to be the vehicles of His power, we can discern the significance of these divers ways, and learn great lessons from them all.

His touch was sometimes obviously the result of what one may venture to call instinctive tenderness, as when He lifted the little children in His arms and laid His hands upon their heads. It was, I suppose, always the spontaneous expression of love and compassion, even when it was something more.

The touch of His hand on the ghastly glossiness of the leper's skin was, no doubt, His assertion of priestly functions, and of elevation above all laws of defilement; but what was it to the poor outcast, who for years had never felt the warm contact of flesh and blood? It always indicated that He Himself was the source of healing and life. It always exprest His identification of Himself with sorrow and sickness. So that it is in principle analogous to, and may be taken as illustrative of, that transcendent act whereby He became flesh, and dwelt among us. Indeed, the very word by which our Lord's taking the blind

man by the hand is described in the chapter
following our text is that employed in the
Epistle to the Hebrews when, dealing with
the true brotherhood of Jesus, the writer says,
"He took not hold of angels, but of the seed
of Abraham he taketh hold." Christ's touch
is His willing contact with man's infirmities
and sins, that He may strengthen and hallow.

And the lesson is one of universal application. Wherever men would help their fellows,
this is a prime requisite, that the would-be
helper should come down to the level of those
whom he desires to aid. If we wish to teach,
we must stoop to think the scholar's thoughts.
The master who has forgotten his boyhood
will have poor success. If we would lead to
purer emotions, we must try to enter into the
lower feelings which we labor to elevate. It
is of no use to stand at the mouth of the al-
leys we wish to cleanse, with our skirts daint-
ily gathered about us, and smelling-bottle in
hand, to preach homilies on the virtue of
cleanliness. We must go in among the filth,
and handle it, if we want to have it cleared
away. The degraded must feel that we do
not shrink from them, or we shall do them no
good. The leper, shunned by all, and ashamed
of himself because everybody loathes him, hun-
gers in his hovel for the grasp of a hand that
does not care for defilement, if it can bring
cleansing. Even in regard to common material helps the principle holds good. We are

too apt to cast our doles to the poor like the
bones to a dog, and then to wonder at what
we are pleased to think men's ingratitude.
A benefit may be so conferred as to hurt more
than a blow; and we cannot be surprised if
so-called charity which is given with contempt
and a sense of superiority, should be received
with a scowl, and chafe a man's spirit like a
fetter. Such gifts bless neither him who gives
nor him who takes. We must put our hearts
into them, if we would win hearts by them.
We must be ready, like our Master, to take
blind beggars by the hand, if we would bless
or help them. The despair and opprobrium
of our modern civilization, the gulf growing
wider and deeper between Dives and Lazarus,
between Belgravia and Whitechapel, the
mournful failure of legalized help, and of
delegated efforts to bridge it over, the darken-
ing ignorance, the animal sensuousness, the
utter heathenism that lives in every town of
England, within a stone's throw of Christian
houses, and near enough to hear the sound of
public worship, will yield to nothing but that
sadly forgotten law which enjoins personal
contact with the sinful and the suffering, as
one chief condition of raising them from the
black mire in which they welter.

The effect of much well-meant Christian effort is simply to irritate. People are very
quick to catch delicate intonations which reveal a secret sense, "how much better, wiser,

more devout I am than these people!'' and
wherever a trace of that appears in our work,
the good of it is apt to be marred. We all
know how hackneyed the charge of spiritual
pride and Pharisaic self-complacency is, and,
thank God, how unjust it often is. But averse
as men may be to the truths which humble,
and willing as they may be to assume that the
very effort to present these to others on our
parts implies a claim which mortifies, we may
at least learn from the threadbare calumny,
what strikes men about our position, and
what rouses their antaganism to us. It is al-
lowable to be taught by our enemies, especially
when it is such a lesson as this, that we must
carefully divest our evangelistic work of apparent pretensions to superiority, and take
our stand by the side of those to whom we
speak. We cannot lecture men into the love
of Christ. We can but win them to it by
showing Christ's love to them; and not the
least important element in that process is the
exhibition of our own love. We have a gospel
to speak of which the very heart is, that the
Son of God stooped to become one with the
lowliest and most sinful; and how can that
gospel be spoken with power unless we, too,
stoop like Him?

We have to echo the invitation, ''Learn of
me, for I am lowly in heart''; and how can
such divine words flow from lips into which
like grace has not been poured? Our theme

is a Savior who shrunk from no sinner, who
gladly consorted with publicans and harlots,
who laid His hand on pollution, and His
heart, full of God and of love, on hearts reek-
ing with sin; and how can our message cor-
respond with our theme if, even in delivering
it, we are saying to ourselves, "The temple of
the Lord are we: this people which knoweth
not the law is curst"? Let us beware of the
very real danger which besets us in this matter, and earnestly seek to make ourselves one
with those whom we would gather into Christ,
by actual familiarity with their condition,
and by identification of ourselves in feeling
with them, after the example of that greatest
of Christian teachers who became "all things
to all men, that by all means he might gain
some"; after the higher example, which Paul
followed, of that dear Lord who, being highest, descended to the lowest, and in the days
of His humiliation was not content with speaking words of power from afar, nor abhorred
the contact of mortality and disease and loath-
some corruption; but laid His hands upon
death, and it lived; upon sickness, and it was
whole; on rotting leprosy, and it was sweet
as the flesh of a little child.

The same principle might be further applied to our Christian work, as affecting the
form in which we should present the truth.
The sympathetic identification of ourselves
with those to whom we try to carry the gospel

will certainly make us wise to know how to shape our message. Seeing with their eyes, we shall be able to graduate the light. Thinking their thoughts, and having in some measure succeeded, by force of sheer community of feeling, in having as it were got inside their minds, we shall unconsciously, and without effort, be led to such aspects of Christ's all-comprehensive truth as they most need. There will be no shooting over people's heads, if we love them well enough to understand them. There will be no toothless generalities, when our interest in men keeps their actual condition and temptations clear before us. There will be no flinging fossil doctrines at them from a height, as if Christ's blest gospel were, in another than the literal sense, "a stone of offense," if we have taken our place on their level. And without such sympathy, these and a thousand other weaknesses and faults will certainly vitiate much of our Christian effort.

We have here the true healing power and the consciousness of wielding it set forth in the Lord's authoritative word.

All the rest of His action was either the spontaneous expression of His true participation in human sorrow, or a merciful veiling of His glory that sense-bound eyes might see it the better. But the word was the utterance of His will, and that was omnipotent. The hand laid on the sick, the blind or the deaf was not even the channel of His power. The

bare putting forth of His energy was all-suf-
ficient. In these we see the loving, pitying
man. In this blazes forth, yet more loving,
yet more compassionate, the effulgence of
manifest God. Therefore so often do we read
the very syllables with which His "voice then
shook the earth," vibrating through all the
framework of the material universe. Therefore do the gospels bid us listen when He rebukes the fever, and it departs; when He says
to the demons, "Go," and they go; when one
word louder in its human articulation than
the howling wind hushes the surges; when
"Talitha cumi" brings back the fair young
spirit from dreary wanderings among the
shades of death. Therefore was it a height
of faith not found in Israel when the Gentile
soldier, whose training had taught him the
power of absolute authority, as heathenism
had driven him to long for a man who would
speak with the imperial sway of a god, recognized in His voice an all-commanding power.
From of old, the very signature of divinity
has been declared to be "He spake, and it
was done"; and He, the breath of whose lips
could set in motion material changes, is that
eternal Word, by whom all things were made.

What unlimited consciousness of sovereign
dominion sounds in that imperative from His
autocratic lips! It is spoken in deaf ears, but
He knows that it will be heard. He speaks
as the fontal source, not as the recipient chan-

nel of healing. He anticipates no delay, no resistance. There is neither effort nor uncertainty in the curt command. He is sure that He has power, and He is sure that the power is His own.

There is no analogy here between us and Him. Alone, fronting the whole race of man, He stands—utterer of a word which none can say after Him, possessor of unshared might, and of His fulness do we all receive. But even from that divine authority and solitary sovereign consciousness we may gather lessons not altogether aside from the purpose of our meeting here to-day. Of His fulness we have received, and the power of the word on His lips may teach us that of His word, even on ours, as the victorious certainty with which He spake His will of healing may remind us of the confidence with which it becomes us to proclaim His name.

His will was almighty then. Is it less mighty or less loving now? Does it not gather all the world in the sweep of its mighty purpose of mercy? His voice pierced then into the dull cold ear of death, and has it become weaker since? His word spoken by Him was enough to banish the foul spirits that run riot, swine-like, in the garden of God in man's soul, trampling down and eating up its flowers and fruitage; is the word spoken of Him less potent to cast them out? Were not all the mighty deeds which He wrought by the breath of His lips on men's bodies prophecies of the yet mightier which His Will of love, and the utterance of that Will by stammering lips, may work on men's souls. Let us not in our faint-heartedness number up our failures, the deaf that will not hear, the dumb that will not speak, His praise; nor unbelievingly say Christ's own word was mighty, but the word concerning Christ is weak on our lips. Not so; our lips are unclean, and our words are weak, but His word—the utterance of His loving will that men should be saved—is what it always was and always will be. We have it, brethren, to proclaim. Did our Master countenance the faithless contrast between the living force of His word when He dwelt on earth, and the feebleness of it as He speaks through His servant? If He did, what did He mean when He said, "He that believeth on me, the works that I do shall he do also, and greater works than these shall he do, because I go unto the Father"?

CROSBY

THE PREPARED WORM

BIOGRAPHICAL NOTE

HOWARD CROSBY, Presbyterian divine, was born in New York City in 1826, educated at New York University, graduating in 1851, was professor of Greek at that institution until 1859, when he was elected to the same chair in Rutgers College. He was pastor of the First Presbyterian Church of New Brunswick, N. J., for the two years ending in 1863, when he assumed charge of the Fourth Avenue Presbyterian Church, New York. From 1870 to 1881 he was chancellor of the University of New York. His activities in the cause of social reform were conspicuous and he exercised his influence in organizing the Society for the Prevention of Crime over which he presided for some years. His energies were also directed against the illegal liquor trade. As a scholar he was prominent among the American revisers of the New Testament and edited a new edition of the "*Oedipus Tyrannus*" of Sophocles. He died in 1891.

CROSBY

1826—1891

THE PREPARED WORM[1]

But God prepared a worm when the morning rose the next day, and it smote the gourd that it withered.— Jonah iv., 7.

JUST when Jonah had felt the delight of the shadowing foliage and had begun to promise himself a most comfortable retreat against an Assyrian sun, the broad-leaved gourd withered. The morning had arrived and the heat was becoming more intense, when the glad shelter was removed, and the prophet's head was smitten with the scorching rays. "It is better for me to die than live," exclaimed the fainting Jonah. And what caused this calamity? A worm. And is that all? No! God prepared the worm. The worm was under orders from heaven, and while he, doubtless, ate into the gourd, with a good appetite, following the bent of his natural constitution, nevertheless he was acting in direct obedience to God. God prepared the worm. And yet in the sixth verse we read that God prepared the gourd. This is the record. "And the Lord God prepared a gourd and made it to come up over

[1] Copyright, 1884, *The Homiletic Review*, New York.

Jonah, that it might be a shadow over his head, to deliver him from his grief. So Jonah was exceedingly glad of the gourd." And then follows immediately: "But God prepared a worm, when the morning rose the next day, and he smote the gourd that it withered." Does God, then, build up in order to destroy? And does He give comfort to His creatures in order to torment them by its removal? So reasons the carnal heart, ready to complain, and looking on all God's conduct in its superficial aspect, its own selfish and sensuous advantage being the criterion of all its judgments. It is an easy counsel of Satan, when we are fainting by a withered gourd. "Curse God and die," the selfish soul is all ripe for such advice,—desperation is more inviting than faith. And there are but few Jobs who can resist the appeal to discontent and anger, in the face of Satan and wife combined, for when the natural depravity of our own hearts is supported by the entreaties of our nearest and dearest friends, hell's heaviest engine is brought against us. "I do well to be angry, even unto death," is the usual style in which we greet the afflictive providence of God. But a faith like Job's, that learns the lesson which the sorrow teaches, is rewarded, as was Job's, by the presence and communion of God, and by a satisfaction with His holy and righteous will.

Let us endeavor to understand some of the

facts connected with our afflictions, as disclosed by the Word of God, in order that we may be prepared to follow Job rather than Jonah.

I. In the first place, God is the author of affliction. "Affliction cometh not forth out of the dust, neither doth trouble spring out of the ground." God asserts most positively in His Word, that all the losses in the world are sent by Him. He calls them chastisements from His fatherly hand. "I make peace and create evil," saith the Lord. This is not evil in the sense of wickedness. God does not create wickedness—but it is evil in the sense of affliction and trouble, the opposite of peace in the contrasted clause, "I make peace and create evil." That is, God is the author equally of prosperity and adversity to His creatures. If it were not so, we should have to imagine certain powers in God's universe not subject to His almighty control, which would be an absurdity. "Shall there be evil in a city and the Lord hath not done it?" It is in this sense of God's hand in adversity that the psalmist cries, "Thou, O God, hast proved us: thou hast tried us as silver is tried; thou broughtest us into the net, thou laidest affliction upon our loins"; and again, "Thy wrath lieth hard upon me, and thou hast afflicted me with all thy waves." God may send affliction by permitting Satan to afflict, but still God is the author of the affliction. He could prevent it, but He permits it. Indeed, it is, perhaps, true that all our losses and injuries in this world are Satan's inflictions, that this ever-active spirit of evil is constantly using the agencies of the natural world for our harm and destruction, and we are preserved simply by the interposing and restraining providence of God. When Satan wished to afflict Job, he sought and gained permission of the Lord. Job's calamities were clearly Satan's blows, and yet Job addresses God, "Why hast thou set me as a mark against thee, so that I am a burden to myself?" So, again, the diseased woman, who heard our Savior's healing words on the Sabbath day and was cured, is described by the same divine Physician (whose diagnosis cannot be questioned) as one whom Satan had bound for eighteen years. Under such examples, I cannot believe we err in attributing all our sicknesses and pains of body to the permitted agency of our arch-adversary.

They are tokens of his power over our race, for he is the prince of this world, and it is only in God that we find protection from his cruel scepter. God suffers us to feel his inflictions in order to remove our affections from the world and to place them more devotedly upon our Heavenly Father. God is thus most truly the author of affliction, whatever may be the agencies He uses in the course of His providence.

II. He uses the natural laws of the world as His agents in afflicting. These laws may be thus used permissively by Satan in other ways than in sickness or not, but the text shows us clearly that God so uses them. ''God prepared a worm.'' There is a world of instruction in that brief statement. It infinitely transcends the science of the naturalist. Bring the most learned explorers of nature together to this gourd of Jonah, and show them this little worm creeping toward the thick stalk. Let them see it move its many feet and flexible body till it reaches the goal of its instinct. Now it uses its gnawing jaws upon the woody fibre; deeper and deeper it pierces the stem; now it reaches the innermost pith, and again returns upon its course. The current of the gourd's life is marred; the leaves droop, and its shelter is gone. Now, ye scientific men, what made that gourd wither? Hear them philosophize. Yon worm is a caterpillar, whose appropriate food is the *ricinus communis*, this very gourd with its palmate leaves and red-tinted flower. The worm has merely followed the impulses of its nature in seeking that tree-like plant, and the equally natural result of its feeding upon the stalk has been the failure of the tree's nourishment, and with the failure the foliage has, of course, withered. Well, is that all science can say? Yes, all. It is little more than that a horse is a horse. It explains nothing but the most proximate causes. It classifies facts, and then leaves us gaping into the abyss of causation as ignorant as ever. Four words from the Bible carry us back to the ultimate cause, the first mover in this gourd's withering. Science talks of laws, but these four words go behind all laws to the Maker of laws, to Him in whose hands are all things. "God prepared a worm." What! says science; drag God in to explain anything? Nay, God drags all in to effect His plans. He has made all things, however great, however small, for Himself. And these things which you call laws are only the methods of His activity, and these methods He has formed for the very ends which He accomplishes by them. The worm which crawls to Jonah's gourd was created by God to destroy that plant, and the law of that worm's movement was ordained for that destruction, as well as for all else which it accomplishes. The mind is satisfied when it finds a mind, a purpose, a plan in every event which it observes, and the pious heart is rejoiced to know that it is a Father's mind and purpose and plan which directs every movement, even to the crawling of a worm. "God prepared a gourd—God prepared a worm"; no accident brought the gourd there; no accident brought the worm there. God stood in a like relation to both. He sent the gourd, through nature, to comfort Jonah. He sent the worm, through nature, to trouble Jonah. Nature is a forlorn object to study unless we find it a mirror to reflect God. It is only as we see it, the result of His handiwork and His instrument in governing His creatures, that nature has a glory. Then it is ennobled; then it has a meaning that no mere naturalist can fathom, but which renders valuable the researches of science with its classifications.

III. God is just in afflicting us. If we look at God simply as the Maker and Owner of His creatures, we could easily deduce His right to afflict. "Is it not lawful for me to do what I will with mine own?" says the Creator; and he must be a daring soul who disputes the force of this question. "Shall the thing formed say to him that formed it, 'Why hast thou made me thus?'" But we are not left to this view of God's right to afflict. God has entered into covenant with us. He has said, "Do ye according to my commandments, and ye shall live." This was the purport of His very first communication to our race in Adam. It treated of obedience and reward, of disobedience and punishment. And what is the record of our race since? Have we obeyed or have we disobeyed? Is there the slightest claim in us for the reward? Is there not the most complete demand for the punishment? What sin in the whole catalog of sin has been omitted by man? Enmity to man and God, pride, ingratitude, and rebellion have marked the history of mankind. And are you and I exceptions? Look at our years of worldliness, years of sinful affections, years of opposition to the Word and Spirit, years of selfishness, and then let us confess our full participation in the general depravity. We are unclean in our natures and by practise, and so, under the covenant which our Maker was pleased to form for us, we can only deserve punishment.

Do we then complain in affliction? Surely, if God would be just in casting us down to hell for our rebellion and disobedience, He is just in laying upon us our earthly afflictions. Shall the Jonah, who ran away from the Lord's commandment, and afterward flung His anger in the face of His God, shall such an one feel that God is unjust in preparing a worm to destroy his gourd? By what arithmetic is such a balance cast? It becomes us, rather, to take up the words of David and cry, "I acknowledge my transgression; and my sin is ever before me. Against thee, thee only, have I sinned and done this evil in thy sight, that thou mightest be justified when thou speakest, and be clear when thou judgest."

IV. God afflicts us in His love. With all Jonah's sins against God, it was not to punish him that God prepared a worm. God is long-suffering and withholds punishment in His desire that all men may come to repentance. If punishment were God's aim in affliction, our afflictions would be infinitely greater than they are, for punishment would be apportioned to desert, and our desert is eternal condemnation; God's aim in affliction is our restoration, our improvement. By it He shakes us off from our dependence upon a world which, however it might please us for the moment, would cheat us sadly in the end. By it He reminds us of Himself as our source of strength and happiness, and then brings us to the unfailing fountain of peace, which our earthly prosperity would hide from our eyes. By it He teaches us to aspire to higher spiritual attainment, to grow in grace, to cultivate a more heavenly disposition of mind and heart.

These are the uses of adversity. Christians who have come through scenes of trial, and whose thankful declaration is, "It was good for me to be afflicted," certify to these blest results. They tell us that they believe nothing else but the severe losses they sustained could have freed them from the fascinations of the world—nothing else could have made holy things so delightful to their soul. Now, such an experience is not the result of God's anger but of God's love. However harsh the voice of God may seem to us, it is yet a Father's voice, with a Father's heart behind it. It is, therefore, meant not to drive us away to seek a hiding corner, but to bring us directly to Himself. The same love which

sent the affliction will receive the afflicted.
God prepares gourds, and God prepares
worms; and He uses each to build up faith
and holiness in the human heart. In earnest
seeking after God, in complete consecration
to His holy will and service, is to be found
the surest avoidance of the worm. If we can
learn our lesson without the worm, the worm
will not be sent to gnaw our gourd to ruins.
The nearer our life to Jesus the more free
shall we be from the sting of affliction. Had
Jonah been an obedient and submissive
prophet his gourd would not have withered.
But alas! Jonah and ourselves need correction
to keep our faces heavenward. Forgetfulness
and indulgence plant their weeds in our
Lord's garden, and they must be rooted up
by force. It is for our own good, and it is
infinite love which decrees it.

Now note some inferences from the subject
under consideration.

First. If God afflicts, how foolish it is to
go to the world for relief? Is the world
greater than God? We may be sure that
any comfort the world can give, as against
God's affliction, must be dangerous. It is a
contest with God, which God may allow to
be successful, but only for the greater condemnation thereafter. The world's relief is
not a cure but an opiate. It stupefies, but
does not give health and strength. The
world's relief is a temporary application—a

lull before a fiercer storm. The world's relief
is a determination not to heed the lesson God
sends us; it is the invention of frivolity, and
not the device of wisdom. More slumber,
more pleasure, and more worldly care are
three favorite medicaments the world uses in
these cases—anodynes which only weaken the
system and prepare it for more fearful suffering. God wishes to awaken the mind by
affliction, and man immediately prescribes a
narcotic. The great Physician brings the affliction for our good; we turn to quackery to
destroy the effects of the divine medicine.
Ah! the day is coming when God shall appear as no longer our Savior but our Judge,
if this be our treatment of His love. ''Because I have called and ye refused; I have
stretched out my hand and no man regarded;
but ye have set at naught all my counsel, and
would none of my reproof; I also will laugh
at your calamity; I will mock when your fear
cometh; when your fear cometh as desolation,
and your destruction cometh as a whirlwind.''

Secondly. If God prepares worms, then
worms at once form an interesting study for
us. We cannot see a caterpillar upon the
leaf, but we know God has a mission for that
worm. He is an ambassador of the Most High
on his way to perform his Master's will. The
headache, which unfits us for our ordinary occupation, is more than a headache. It is the
voice of our God. Let us listen to the next

headache and hear what God would have us learn. Every bird and beast, every raindrop and sunbeam, every breath of wind, and every event, however small, are the writings of a heavenly scribe. Let us study God's providence. It is all a message of love to us. We shall find out infinitely more in this study than in deciphering the hieroglyphics of Egypt. We shall find correction, expostulation, comfort, encouragement and instruction; and the more we look, the more we shall see. We shall become adepts in the high art of interpreting the acts of God toward us, and in this, as in prayer, hold constant communion with our divine Redeemer.

Thirdly. When our gourds wither it is a proof that God is near. We should be ready to say with Jacob, "Surely the Lord is in this place." Prayer and humiliation are now our appropriate exercises. God has put forth His hand to summon us to these duties. Our gourd is gone, but our God is not gone, He can protect far better than a gourd. He will more than make up all our losses. Let us go to Him, and our dark night will make the day-dawn more brilliant. My dying fellow-sinner, do not, I beseech you, grow angry under God's severe dispensations. You do not well to be angry. God is near you with a blessing in His hand for you. He has a lesson for you to learn which will make you wise unto salvation.

Say, will you learn it? If not, God is near you to condemn you. Oh! dread the alternative, and be wise to say in your heart, "Blest be my God and Father, who prepared the worm to destroy my broad-leaved gourd!"

DALE

THE ARGUMENT FROM EXPERIENCE

BIOGRAPHICAL NOTE

ROBERT WILLIAM DALE was born in London, England, in 1829 and died in 1895. His long and fruitful ministry was confined to Birmingham, where he preached with great power. He believed, as he once said, that if a minister had anything from God to say to his fellow men, they would gladly come to hear him. He favored extemporaneous preaching, was a devoted student of English style, and advocated in his Yale lectures a more thorough attention to this important subject. He said:

"There is no reason why, when you have at your service the noblest language for an orator that was ever spoken by the human race, you should be satisfied with the threadbare phrases, the tawdry, tarnished finery, the patched and ragged garments, with the smell like that of the stock of a second-hand clothes shop, with which half-educated and ambitious declaimers are content to cover the nakedness of their thought. You can do something better than this, and you should resolve to do it."

DALE
1829—1895

THE ARGUMENT FROM EXPERIENCE[1]

THERE are large numbers of people who suppose that modern science and modern criticism have destroyed the foundations of faith, and who can not understand how it is possible, in these days, for intelligent, open-minded, educated men to believe in the Lord Jesus Christ.

There are many persons who are convinced that the ascertained conclusions of modern science and of modern criticism are destructive of the authority which has been attributed both to the Jewish and the Christian Scriptures, that the traditional opinions concerning the authorship and the dates of many of the books of the Old Testament are false; and that most of the writings contained in the New Testament are spurious. Or, if some of the extreme conclusions of the destructive criticism are not regarded as finally established, it is known that great names can be quoted for, as well as against, them. And as it is assumed that the Jewish and the Christian Scriptures are the foundations of Chris-

[1] Reprinted by permission of Messrs. A. C. Armstrong & Son.

tian faith, that we must believe in the genuineness and historical trustworthiness of these ancient books, and even in their inspiration, before we can believe in Christ, they argue that, until these discussions are finally closed in favor of the traditional opinions, faith in Christ is impossible. The controversies have not, in any large number of cases, destroyed faith where faith already existed; but where faith does not exist, they appear to very many persons to create an insuperable obstacle to faith.

To such persons, if they are serious and well informed, there is something perplexing in the persistency of the faith of the great majority of Christian believers. Among those who remain Christian there are men whose intellectual vigor, patience, and keenness are equal to their own; men who are their equals in general intellectual culture, and who know as much as they know about the currents of modern thought; candid men; men who are incorruptible in their loyalty to truth; men who have a due sense of the immense importance, in relation to the higher life of the human race, of the questions at issue:

How is it that the faith in Christ of such men is unshaken?

The substance of the answer that I make here to the question, why it is that those who believe in Christ continue to believe, may be given in a single sentence: Whatever may have been the original grounds of their faith, their faith has been verified in their own personal experience.

They have trusted in Christ for certain great and wonderful things, and they have received great and wonderful things. They have not perhaps received precisely what they expected when their Christian life began, for the kingdom of heaven cannot be really known until a man has entered into it; but what they have received assures them that Christ is alive, that He is within reach, and that He is the Savior and Lord of men.

That they have received these blessings in answer to their faith in Christ is a matter of personal consciousness. They know it, as they know that fire burns.

Their experience varies. Some of them would say they can recall acts of Christ in which His personal volition and His supernatural power were as definitely manifested as in any of the miracles recorded in the four Gospels. They were struggling unsuccessfully with some evil temper—with envy, jealousy, personal ambition—and could not subdue it. They hated it; they hated themselves for being under its tyranny; but expel it they could not. If it seemed supprest for a time, it returned; and returned with its malignant power increased rather than diminished. They scourged themselves with scorpions for yielding to it; still they yielded. In their despair they appealed to Christ; and in a moment the evil fires were quenched, and they were never rekindled. These instantaneous deliverances are perhaps exceptional; but to those who can recall them they carry an irresistible conviction that the living Christ has heard their cry and answered them.

The more ordinary experiences of the Christian life, tho less striking, are not less conclusive. The proof that Christ has heard prayer is not always concentrated into a moment, but is more commonly spread over large tracts of time. Prayer is offered for an increase of moral strength in resisting temptation, or for the disappearance of reluctance in the discharge of duties which are distasteful, or for a more gracious and kindly temper, or for patience and courage in bearing trouble, or for self-control, or for relief from exhausting and fruitless anxiety; and the answer comes. It comes gradually, but still it comes. We had lost hope. It seemed as if all our moral vigor was dying down, and as if nothing could restore it. The tide was slowly ebbing, and we were powerless to recall the retreating waters; but after we prayed it ceased to ebb; for a time it seemed stationary; then it began to flow; and tho with many of us it has never reached the flood, the wholesome waters have renewed the energy and the joy of life.

Or we prayed to Christ to liberate us from

some evil habit. The chains did not fall away at His touch, like the chains of Peter at the touch of the angel; but in some mysterious way they were loosened, and at the same time we received accessions of strength. The old habit continued to trouble us; it still impeded our movements: but we could move; we recovered some measure of freedom, and were conscious that we were slaves no longer. There still remained a mechanical and automatic tendency to the evil ways of thinking, speaking, or acting; but we had become vigilant and alert, and were prompt to resist the tendency as soon as it began to work; and we were strong enough to master it. In the course of time the tendency became weaker and weaker, and at last, in some cases, it almost disappeared.

Some men have appealed to Christ when they have been seized with a great horror through the discovery of their guilt. It was not the awful penalty which menaces the impenitent that haunted and terrified them. Nor was their distress occasioned chiefly by the consciousness of moral evil. They feared the penalty, and they were humiliated and shamed by the contrast between ideal goodness and their own moral and spiritual life; but what stung and tortured them, sunk them into despair, filled heaven and earth with a darkness that could be felt, and made life intolerable, was their guilt—guilt which they had incurred by their past sins, and which they continued to incur by their present sinfulness.

When once this sense of guilt fastens itself on a man, he cannot shake it off at will. The keen agony may gradually pass into a dull, dead pain; and after a time, the sensibility of the soul may seem to be wholly lost; but a man can never be sure that the horror will not return.

The real nature of this experience is best seen when it has been occasioned by the grosser and more violent forms of crime. Men who have committed murder, for example, have been driven almost insane by the memory of their evil deed. Their agony may have had nothing in it of the nature of repentance; they were not distrest because their crime had revealed to them the malignity and the fierce strength of their passions; they had no desire to become gentle and kindly. They were filled with horror and remorse by their awful guilt. They felt that the crime was theirs, and would always continue to be theirs; that it would be theirs if it remained concealed as truly as if it were known; indeed, it seemed to be in some terrible way more truly theirs so long as the secret was kept. It was not the fear of punishment that convulsed them; they have sometimes brought on themselves public indignation and abhorrence, and have condemned themselves to the gallows by confess-

ing their crime in order to obtain relief from
their agony.

Suppose that a man possest by this great
horror discovered that, in some wonderful
way, the dark and damning stain on his conscience had disappeared; that, altho he had
done the deed, the iron chain which bound
him to the criminality of it had been broken;
that before God and man and his own conscience he was free from the guilt of it;—the
supposition, in its completeness, is an impossible one; but if it were possible, the discovery
would lift the man out of the darkness of hell
into the light of heaven.

But to large numbers of Christian men a
discovery which in substance is identical with
this has actually come in response to their
trust in Christ. Nothing is more intensely
real than the sense of guilt; it is as real as
the eternal distinction between right and
wrong in which it is rooted. And nothing is
more intensely real than the sense of release
from guilt which comes from the discovery
and assurance of the remission of sins. The
evil things which a man has done cannot be
undone; but when they have been forgiven
through Christ, the iron chain which so bound
him to them as to make the guilt of them
eternally his has been broken; before God
and his own conscience he is no longer guilty
of them. This is the Christian mystery of jus-
tification, which, according to Paul—and his

words have been confirmed in the experience of millions of Christian men—is "the power of God unto salvation to every one that believeth." It changes darkness into light; despair into victorious hope; prostration into buoyancy and vigor. It is one of the supreme motives to Christian living, and it makes Christian living possible. The man who has received this great deliverance is no longer a convict, painfully observing all prison rules with the hope of shortening his sentence, but a child in the home of God.

There are experiences of another kind by which the faith of Christian men is verified. Of these one of the most decisive and most wonderful is the consciousness that through Christ he has passed into the eternal and divine order. He belongs to two worlds. He is just as certain that he is environed by things unseen and eternal as that he is environed by things seen and temporal. In the power of the life given to him in the new birth he has entered into the kingdom of God. He is conscious that that diviner region is now the native land of his soul. It is there that he finds perfect rest and perfect freedom. It is a relief to escape to its eternal peace and glory from the agitations and vicissitudes, the sorrows and successes, of this transitory world. It is not always that he is vividly conscious of belonging to that eternal order; this supreme blessedness is reserved for the great hours of life; but he knows that it lies about him always, and that at any moment the great Apocalypse may come. And even when it is hidden, its "powers" continue to act upon him, as the light and heat of the sun pass through the clouds by which the burning splendor is softened and concealed.

Further, "in Christ" Christian men know God; they know Him for themselves. The mere conception of God is as different from the immediate knowledge of Him as the mere conception of the Matterhorn from the actual vision of it as an external objective grandeur; and it is not the conception of God, but God Himself, that fills them with awe and wonder, and with a blessedness which trembles into devout fear. Sometimes the "exceeding weight of glory" is too great to bear, and human infirmity is relieved when the vision passes. At other times God is more than a transcendent glory to be contemplated and adored. His infinite love, to use Paul's words, is shed abroad in their hearts, like the sun's heat under tropical heavens; it is immediately revealed. How, they can not tell, any more than they can tell how the material world is revealed to sense; they only know that, apart from any self-originated effort, apart from any movement of their own towards Him, the eternal Spirit draws near to their spirit and reveals God's love to them. It is as if the warm streams of the love which have their fountains in the depths of His infinite life were flowing round them and into them. They are conscious of that love for them of which God is conscious.

And this blessedness is not the prerogative of elect saints, or of those who may be said to have a natural genius for spiritual thought. It is the common inheritance of all that are "in Christ," altho there is reason to fear that many Christian people rarely reach the height of its joy. But among those who reach it are men of every degree of intellectual rank and every variety of moral and spiritual temperament. It is reached by ignorant men, whose thoughts are narrow and whose minds are inert, as well as by men with large knowledge and great powers of speculation; by men destitute of imagination, as well as by men whose imagination kindles as soon as it is touched by the splendors of nature or by the verses of poets. Men whose life moves slowly and sluggishly reach it, as well as men who are impulsive, ardent, and adventurous. And where this experience is known, it becomes an effective force in the moral life. Peter, writing to slaves, says, "For this is acceptable, if through consciousness of God a man endureth griefs, suffering wrongfully."

I have said that "in Christ" men know God—not merely through Christ. It is true that during His earthly ministry He revealed God; so that, in answer to the prayer of one of His disciples, "Show us the Father, and it sufficeth us," He said, "Have I been so long time with you, and dost thou not know me, Philip? he that hath seen me hath seen the Father." That revelation has eternal power and value; but there are other words spoken by Christ that same night which suggest that it is not merely by the revelation of God during His earthly ministry that Christ has made it possible for men to know the Father. He said: "I am the true vine, and ye are the branches. . . . Abide in me, and I in you. As the branch cannot bear fruit of itself, except it abide in the vine; so neither can ye, except ye abide in me. He that abideth in me, and I in him, the same beareth much fruit: for apart from me ye can do nothing." It is not certain that when Paul wrote his Epistle to the Galatian Christians he had heard of these words; but what they meant he had learnt for himself. He said, "I live: and yet no longer I, but Christ liveth in me." In various measures the experience of Paul has been the experience of Christian men ever since. Their relationship to Christ—their conscious relationship to Christ—has been most mysterious, but most intimate and most certain. They have meditated on the infinite love which moved Him to descend from the heights of God and to become man, upon His graciousness and gentleness, His purity, His spontaneous goodness, His pity for suffering,

His merciful words to the sinful, His patience and His long-suffering, and His fiery indignation against hypocrisy; they have meditated on His teaching, on all the words of His that have been preserved concerning the love and grace of God, concerning the remission of sins, the gift of eternal life, the judgment to come, the eternal blessedness of the righteous, and the doom of the lost; they have felt the spell and the charm of that ideal perfection to which He calls them in His precepts, and which He illustrated and transcended in His own character: but they have been conscious that it was not merely by the power of the great and pathetic story of His earthly history, or by the power of His spiritual and ethical teaching, that He gives to men the life of God, and constantly renews, sustains, and augments it. They shared the very life of their Lord. He lived in them. They lived in Him. And it was in the power of this common life that they knew God.

Nor is it only the immediate knowledge of God that is rendered possible by this union with Christ. Christian men are conscious that they do not receive strength from Christ for common duty, as they might receive strength from One who, while He conferred the grace, stood apart from them, but that in some wonderful way they are strong in the strength of Christ Himself. They are too often drawn down into the region of baser forces, and then

116

they fall; but their very failure verifies the truth of their happier experiences, for it brings home to them afresh what they are apart from Christ; and when they recover their union with Him—which indeed had not been lost, tho for a time it was not realized— they recover their power.

The man who has had, and who still has, such experiences as these will listen with great tranquillity to criticisms which are intended to shake the historical credit of the four Gospels, altho the story they contain may have been the original ground of his faith in Christ. The criticism may be vigorous; he may be wholly unable to answer it: but what then? Is he to cease to believe in Christ? Why should he?

Let me answer these questions by an illustration. Towards the close of our Lord's ministry, when He was in the neighborhood of Jericho—just leaving the city or just entering it—Bartimeus, a blind man, who was begging at the side of the road, heard that Jesus of Nazareth was passing by, and He appealed to the great Prophet to have mercy upon him. Jesus answered his appeal, and gave him sight. Now it is possible that Bartimeus may have been told by some passing traveler, of whom he knew nothing, the story of a similar miracle which Jesus had worked a few weeks before in Jerusalem, and this may have been the ground, and the only ground, of his confidence in our Lord's supernatural power. If, after he had received his sight, some sagacious friend of his had asked him how it was that he came to believe that the Nazarene Teacher could give sight to the blind, nothing would have been easier than for his friend to show that, whether the story of the Jerusalem miracle was true or not, Bartimeus had no trustworthy evidence of its truth. A tale told by an unknown stranger! This was no sufficient reason for believing that Jesus had given sight to a man born blind. Did the stranger who told the tale know the beggar who was said to have been cured? Was it certain that the man was blind? Had the stranger examined his eyes the very morning of the day on which he received sight? Was it certain that the vision was not gradually returning? Was the stranger present when Jesus made the clay, and put it on the blind man's eyes; close enough to see that no delicate operation was performed during the process? The sending of the blind man to wash at the Pool of Siloam was suspicious: what could that washing have to do with a miracle? Did the stranger go with the man to the pool, and keep his eye upon him while he was there? Was it quite certain that the blind beggar who was sent to Siloam was the man who came back to the city and declared that Jesus had healed him? Might not one man have been sent to the pool, and another man have come back to Jerusalem? It looked very much as if there were some previous understanding between the blind man and the Nazarene Prophet. The Prophet had rich friends; they could have made it worth the man's while to come into the plot. Had Bartimeus considered all these difficulties? Was it not more probable that the stranger's story should be false than that the miracle should be true? Would it not be well for Bartimeus to suspend his faith in Jesus until he had made further inquiries about the miracle?

We can imagine the answer of Bartimeus. I think that he would have said: "At first I believed in the power of Jesus of Nazareth, because I was told that He had given sight to another blind man; now I am sure of His power, because He has given sight to me. It is possible, as you say, that the story about the blind man in Jerusalem is not true. You have asked me many questions which I can not answer. I can not explain why he should have been sent to the Pool of Siloam. I acknowledge that the evidence which I have for the miracle is not decisive. As Jesus has restored my sight, I think that the story is probably true; but whether the story is true or not can not disturb my faith in Him, for if He did not heal the other man, He has healed me."

And so the faith in the living Christ of those who have had the great experiences of

His power and grace which I have described is not shaken by any assaults on the historical trustworthiness of the story of His earthly ministry. Much less can it be shaken by discussions concerning the nature and origin of the ancient Scriptures of the Jewish people. Their confidence in the books, both of the Old Testament and the New, may perhaps have to be suspended until the controversies of scholars are closed, or until, on historical and critical grounds, they can see their own way to firm and definite conclusions about the main questions at issue; but not their confidence in Christ. They may be uncertain about the books; they are sure about Him. Both Christian scholars and the commonalty of Christian people approach the controversies on these ancient records with a settled faith in the power and grace and glory of Christ. Their faith in Him rests on foundations which lie far beyond the reach of scientific and historical criticism. They know for themselves that Christ is the Savior of men: for they have received through Him the remission of their own sins; He has translated them into the divine kingdom; He has given them strength for righteousness, and through Him they have found God.

THE WORLD'S GREAT SERMONS

LIDDON

INFLUENCES OF THE HOLY SPIRIT

BIOGRAPHICAL NOTE

HENRY PARRY LIDDON was born at North Stoneham, Hampshire, in 1829. His intellectual power and fearless and earnest preaching attracted immense congregations to St. Paul's Cathedral, London. He sought to meet the speculative fallacies of his day by truth clearly and boldly proclaimed. Probably his greatest fault in delivery was that he tied himself slavishly to a manuscript in all his preaching. There was a force and intensity to his delivery, however, that often projected his words towards his hearers like great projectiles across a battlefield. Dr. Arthur S. Hoyt recommends him for study in these words: " Canon Liddon brings the riches of exegesis and theology and philosophy to the pulpit, and gives to the sermon the distinction of his refined and spiritual personality." He died in 1890.

LIDDON

1829—1890

INFLUENCES OF THE HOLY SPIRIT

*The wind bloweth where it listeth, and thou hearest the
sound thereof, but canst not tell whence it cometh, and
whither it goeth.*—St. John iii., 8.

WHO has not felt the contrast, the almost tragic contrast, between the
high station of the Jewish doctor,
member of the Sanhedrin, master in Israel,
and the ignorance of elementary religious
truth, as we Christians must deem it, which
he displayed in this interview with our blest
Lord? At first sight it seems difficult to understand how our Lord could have used the
simile in the text when conversing with an
educated and thoughtful man, well conversed
in the history and literature of God's ancient
people; and, indeed, a negative criticism has
availed itself of this and of some other features in the narrative, in the interest of the
theory that Nicodemus was only a fictitious
type of the higher classes in Jewish society, as
they were pictured to itself by the imagination of the fourth Evangelist. Such a supposition, opposed to external facts and to all
internal probabilities, would hardly have been
entertained, if the critical ingenuity of its au-

thor had been seconded by any spiritual experience. Nicodemus is very far from being a caricature; and our Lord's method here, as elsewhere, is to lead on from familiar phrases and the well-remembered letter to the spirit and realities of religion. The Jewish schools were acquainted with the expression "a new creature"; but it had long since become a mere shred of official rhetoric. As applied to a Jewish proselyte, it scarcely meant more than a change in the outward relations of religious life. Our Lord told Nicodemus that every man who would see the kingdom of God which He was founding must undergo a second birth; and Nicodemus, who had been accustomed to the phrase all his life, could not understand it if it was to be supposed to mean anything real. "How," he asks, "can a man be born when he is old? Can he enter a second time into his mother's womb, and be born?" Our Lord does not extricate him from this blundering literalism; He repeats His own original assertion, but in terms which more fully express His meaning: "Verily, verily, I say unto thee, Except a man be born of water and of the Spirit, he can not enter into the kingdom of God. That which is born of the flesh is flesh; and that which is born of the Spirit is spirit. Marvel not that I said unto thee, Ye must be born again." Our Lord's reference to water would not have been unintelligible to Nicodemus; every one in

Judæa knew that the Baptist had insisted on immersion in water as a symbol of the purification of the soul of man. Certainly, in connecting "water" with the Spirit and the new birth, our Lord's language, glancing at that of the prophet, went very far beyond this. He could only be fully understood at a later time, when the sacrament of baptism had been instituted, just as the true sense of His early allusions to His death could not have been apprehended until after the crucifixion. But Nicodemus, it is plain, had not yet advanced beyond his original difficulty; he could not conceive how any second birth was possible, without altogether violating the course of nature. And our Lord penetrates His thoughts and answers them. He answers them by pointing to that invisible agent who could achieve, in the sphere of spiritual and mental life, what the Jewish doctor deemed so impossible a feat as a second birth. Nature, indeed, contained no force that could compass such a result; but nature in this, as in other matters, was a shadow of something beyond itself.

It was late at night when our Lord had this interview with the Jewish teacher. At the pauses in conversation, we may conjecture, they heard the wind without as it moaned along the narrow streets of Jerusalem; and our Lord, as was His wont, took His creature into His service—the service of spiritual truth. The wind was a figure of the Spirit. Our Lord would not have used the same word for both. The wind might teach Nicodemus something of the action of Him who is the real Author of the new birth of man. And it would do this in two ways more especially.

On a first survey of nature, the wind arrests man's attention, as an unseen agent which seems to be moving with entire freedom. "The wind bloweth where it listeth." It is fettered by none of those conditions which confine the swiftest bodies that traverse the surface of the earth; it sweeps on as if independent of law, rushing hither and thither, as tho obeying its own wayward and momentary impulse. Thus it is an apt figure of a self-determining invisible force; and of a force which is at times of overmastering power. Sometimes, indeed, its breath is so gentle, that only a single leaf or blade of grass will at distant intervals seem to give the faintest token of its action; yet, even thus, it "bloweth where it listeth." Sometimes it bursts upon the earth with destructive violence; nothing can resist its onslaught; the most solid buildings give way; the stoutest trees bend before it; whatever is frail and delicate can only escape by the completeness of its submission. Thus, too, it "bloweth where it listeth." Beyond anything else that strikes upon the senses of man, it is suggestive of free supersensuous power; it is an appropriate symbol of an irruption of the invisible into the world of sense, of the action, so tender or so imperious, of the divine and eternal Spirit upon the human soul.

But the wind is also an agent about whose proceedings we really know almost nothing. "Thou hearest the sound thereof"; such is our Lord's concession to man's claim to knowledge. "Thou canst not tell whence it cometh, and whither it goeth"; such is the reserve which He makes in respect of human ignorance. Certainly we do more than hear the sound of the wind; its presence is obvious to three of the senses. We feel the chill or the fury of the blast; and, as it sweeps across the ocean, or the forest, or the field of corn, we see how the blades rise and fall in graceful curves, and the trees bend, and the waters sink and swell into waves which are the measure of its strength. But our Lord says, "Thou hearest the sound thereof." He would have us test it by the most spiritual of the senses. It whispers, or it moans, or it roars as it passes us; it has a pathos all its own. Yet what do we really know about it? "Thou canst not tell whence it cometh, and whither it goeth." Does the wind then obey no rule; is it a mere symbol of unfettered caprice? Surely not. If, as the psalmist sings, "God bringeth the winds out of his treasuries," He acts, we may be sure, here as always, whether in nature or in grace, by some law,

which his own perfections impose upon His
action. He may have given to us of these
later times to see a very little deeper beneath
the surface of the natural world than was the
case with our fathers. Perchance we explain
the immediate antecedents of the phenomenon; but can we explain our own explanation?
The frontier of our ignorance is removed one
stage farther back; but "the way of the
wind" is as fitting an expression for the mysteries now as it was in the days of Solomon.
We know that there is no cave of Æolus. We
know that the wind is the creature of that
great Master who works everywhere and in-
cessantly by rule. But, as the wind still
sweeps by us who call ourselves the children
of an age of knowledge, and we endeavor to
give our fullest answer to the question,
"Whence it cometh, and whither it goeth?"
we discover that, as the symbol of a spiritual
force, of whose presence we are conscious,
while we are unable to determine, with mod-
erate confidence, either the secret principle
or the range of its action, the wind is as full
of meaning still as in the days of Nicodemus.

When our Lord has thus pointed to the freedom and the mysteriousness of the wind, He
adds, "So is every one that is born of the
Spirit." The simile itself would have led
us to expect—"So is the Spirit of God."
The man born of the Spirit would answer not
to the wind itself, but to the sensible effect

of the wind. There is a break of corre-
spondence between the simile and its application. The simile directs attention to
the divine Author of the new birth in
man. The words which follow direct attention to the human subject upon whom the
divine agent works. Something similar is
observable when our Lord compares the kingdom of heaven to a merchantman seeking
goodly pearls; the kingdom really corresponds
not to the merchantman, but to the pearl of
great price which the merchantman buys. In
such cases, we may be sure, the natural cor-
respondence between a simile and its application is not disturbed without a motive. And
the reason for this disturbance is presumably
that the simile is not adequate to the full purpose of the speaker, who is anxious to teach
some larger truth than its obvious application
would suggest. In the case before us, we may
be allowed to suppose, that by His reference
to the wind our Lord desired to convey something more than the real but mysterious
agency of the Holy Spirit in the new birth of
man. His language seems designed, not merely to correct the materialistic narrowness of
the Jewish doctor, not merely to answer by
anticipation the doubts of later days as to the
spiritual efficacy of His own sacrament of
regeneration, but to picture, in words which
should be read to the end of time, the general
work of that divine person whose mission of

mercy to our race was at once the consequence and the completion of His own.

It may be useful to trace the import of our Lord's simile in three fields of the action of the holy and eternal Spirit; His creation of a sacred literature, His guidance of a divine society, and His work upon individual souls.

I. As, then, we turn over the pages of the Bible, must we not say, "The wind of heaven bloweth where it listeth"? If we might reverently imagine ourselves scheming beforehand what kind of a book the Book of God ought to be, how different would it be from the actual Bible. There would be as many bibles as there are souls, and they would differ as widely. But in one thing, amid all their differences, they would probably agree; they would lack the variety, both in form and substance, of the holy Book which the Church of God places in the hands of her children. The self-assertion, the scepticism, and the fastidiousness of our day would meet like the men of the second Roman triumvirate on that island in the Reno, and would draw up their lists of proscription. One would condemn the poetry of Scripture as too inexact; another its history as too largely secular; another its metaphysics as too transcendental, or as hostile to some fanciful ideal of "simplicity," or as likely to quench a purely moral enthusiasm. The archaic history of the Pentateuch, or the sterner side of the ethics of the psalter, or the

supernaturalism of the histories of Elijah or
of Daniel, or the so-called pessimism of Eccle-
siastes, or the alleged secularism of Esther, or
the literal import of the Song of Solomon,
would be in turn condemned. Nor could the
apostles hope to escape: St. John would be
too mystical in this estimate; St. James too
legal in that; St. Paul too dialectical, or too
metaphysical, or too easily capable of an an-
tinomian interpretation; St. Peter too unde-
cided, as if balancing between St. Paul and
St. James. Our new Bible would probably be
uniform, narrow, symmetrical; it would be
entirely made up of poetry, or of history, or
of formal propositions, or of philosophical
speculation, or of lists of moral maxims; it
would be modeled after the type of some current writer on English history, or some popular poet or metaphysician, or some sentimen-
talist who abjures history and philosophy
alike on principle, or some composer of well-
intentioned religious tracts for general cir-
culation. The inspirations of heaven would
be taken in hand, and instead of a wind blow-
ing where it listeth, we should have a wind,
no doubt, of some kind, rustling earnestly
enough along some very narrow crevices or
channels, in obedience to the directions of
some one form of human prejudice, or passion, or fear, or hope.

The Bible is like nature in its immense, its
exhaustless variety; like nature, it reflects all

the higher moods of the human soul, because
it does much more; because it brings us face
to face with the infinity of the divine life.
In the Bible the wind of heaven pays scant
heed to our anticipations or our prejudices;
it "bloweth where it listeth." It breathes not
only in the divine charities of the gospels,
not only in the lyrical sallies of the epistles,
not only in the great announcements scattered
here and there in Holy Scripture of the magnificence, or the compassion, or the benevolence of God; but also in the stern language
of the prophets, in the warnings and lessons
of the historical books, in the revelations of
divine justice and of human responsibility
which abound in either Testament. "Where
it listeth." Not only where our sense of literary beauty is stimulated, as in St. Paul's picture of charity, by lines which have taken cap-
tive the imagination of the world, not only
where feeling and conscience echo the verdict
of authority and the promptings of reverence,
but also where this is not the case; where
neither precept nor example stimulates us, and
we are left face to face with historical or ethical material, which appears to us to inspire no
spiritual enthusiasm, or which is highly suggestive of critical difficulty. Let us be patient;
we shall understand, if we will only wait, how
these features of the Bible too are integral
parts of a living whole; here, as elsewhere,
the Spirit breathes; in the genealogies of the

Chronicles as in the last discourse in St. John, though with an admitted difference of manner and degree. He "bloweth where He listeth." The apostle's words respecting the Old Testament are true of the New: "All Scripture is given by inspiration of God, and is profitable for doctrine, for reproof, for correction, for instruction in righteousness." And, "Whatsoever things were written aforetime were written for our learning, that we through patience and comfort of the Scriptures might have hope."

"But thou hearest the sound thereof, and canst not tell whence it cometh, and whither it goeth." The majesty of Scripture is recognized by man, wherever there is, I will not say a spiritual faculty, but a natural sense of beauty. The "sound" of the wind is perceived by the trained ear, by the literary taste, by the refinement, by the humanity of every generation of educated men. But what beyond? What of its spiritual source, its spiritual drift and purpose, its half-concealed but profound unities, its subtle but imperious relations to conscience? Of these things, so precious to Christians, a purely literary appreciation of Scripture is generally ignorant; the sacred Book, like the prophet of the Chebar, is only "as a very lovely song of one that hath a pleasant voice, and can play well on an instrument." Or again, the "sound thereof" is heard in the admitted empire of

the Bible over millions of hearts and consciences; an empire the evidences of which
strike upon the ear in countless ways, and
which is far too wide and too secure to be
affected by the criticisms that might occasion-
ally seem to threaten it. What is the secret
of this influence of Scripture? Not simply
that it is the Book of Revelation; since it contains a great deal of matter which lay fairly
within the reach of man's natural faculties.
The Word or eternal Reason of God is the
Revealer; but Scripture, whether it is a record
of divine revelations or of naturally observed
facts, is, in the belief of the Christian Church,
throughout "inspired" by the Spirit. Inspiration is the word which describes the presence and action of the Holy Spirit everywhere
in Scripture. We know not how our own
spirits, hour by hour, are acted upon by the
eternal Spirit, though we do not question the
fact; we content ourselves with recognizing
what we can not explain. If we believe that
Scripture is inspired, we know that it is instinct with the presence of Him whose voice
we might hear in every utterance, but of
whom we cannot tell whence He cometh or
whither He goeth.

II. The history of the Church of Christ
from the days of the apostles has been a history of spiritual movements. Doubtless it has
been a history of much else; the Church has
been the scene of human passions, human

speculations, human errors. But traversing these, He by whom the whole body of the Church is governed and sanctified, has made His presence felt, not only in the perpetual proclamation and elucidation of truth, not only in the silent, never-ceasing sanctification of souls, but also in great upheavals of spiritual life, by which the conscience of Christians has been quickened, or their hold upon the truths of redemption and grace made more intelligent and serious, or their lives and practise restored to something like the ideal of the Gospels. Even in the apostolic age it was necessary to warn Christians that it was high time to awake out of sleep; that the night of life was far spent, and the day of eternity was at hand. And ever since, from generation to generation, there has been a succession of efforts within the Church to realize more worthily the truth of the Christian creed, or the ideal of the Christian life. These revivals have been inspired or led by devoted men who have represented the highest conscience of Christendom in their day. They may be traced along the line of Christian history; the Spirit living in the Church has by them attested His presence and His will; and has recalled lukewarm generations, paralyzed by indifference or degraded by indulgence, to the true spirit and level of Christian faith and life.

In such movements there is often what

seems, at first sight, an element of caprice. They appear to contemporaries to be one-sided, exaggerated, narrow, fanatical. They are often denounced with a passionate fervor which is so out of proportion to the reality as to border on the grotesque. They are said to exact too much of us, or to concede too much. They are too contemplative in their tendency to be sufficiently practical, or too energetically practical to do justice to religious thought. They are too exclusively literary and academical, as being the work of men of books; or they are too popular and insensible to philosophical considerations, as being the work of men of the people. Or, again, they are so occupied with controversy as to forget the claims of devotion, or so engaged in leading souls to a devout life as to forget the unwelcome but real necessities of controversy. They are intent on particular moral improvements so exclusively as to forget what is due to reverence and order; or they are so bent upon rescuing the Church from chronic slovenliness and indecency in public worship as to do less than justice to the paramount interests of moral truth. Sometimes these movements are all feeling; sometimes they are all thought; sometimes they are, as it seems, all outward energy. In one age they produce a literature like that of the fourth and fifth centuries; in another they found orders of men devoted to preaching or to works of

mercy, as in the twelfth; in another they
enter the lists, as in the thirteenth century,
with a hostile philosophy; in another they attempt a much-needed reformation of the
Church; in another they pour upon the
heathen world a flood of light and warmth
from the heart of Christendom. It is easy,
as we survey them, to say that something else
was needed; or that what was done could
have been done better or more completely;
or that, had we been there, we should not have
been guilty of this onesidedness, or of that
exaggeration. We forget, perhaps, who really
was there, and whose work it is, though often
overlaid and thwarted by human weakness
and human passion, that we are really criti-
cizing. If it was seemingly onesided, exces-
sive or defective, impulsive or sluggish, speculative or practical, esthetic or experimental,
may not this have been so because in His
judgment, who breatheth where He listeth,
this particular characteristic was needed for
the Church of that day? All that contemporaries know of such movements is "the sound
thereof"; the names with which they are associated, the controversies which they precipi-
tate, the hostilities which they rouse or allay,
as the case may be. Such knowledge is superficial enough; of the profound spiritual
causes which really engender them, of the direction in which they are really moving, of
the influence which they are destined perma-

nently to exert upon souls, men know little or nothing. The accidental symptom is mistaken for the essential characteristic; the momentary expression of feeling for the inalienable conviction of certain truth. The day may come, perhaps, when more will be known; when practise and motive, accident and substance, the lasting and the transient, will be seen in their true relative proportions; but for the time this can hardly be. He is passing by, whose way is in the sea, and His paths in the deep waters, and His footsteps unknown. The Eternal Spirit is passing; and men can only say, "He bloweth where He listeth."

III. Our Lord's words apply especially to Christian character. There are some effects of the living power of the Holy Spirit which are invariable. When He dwells with a Christian soul, He continually speaks in the voice of conscience; He speaks in the voice of prayer. He produces with the ease of a natural process, without effort, without the taint of self-consciousness, "love, joy, peace, long-suffering, gentleness, goodness, faith, meekness, temperance." Some of these graces must be found where He makes His home. There is no mistaking the atmosphere of His presence: in its main features it is the same now as in the days of the apostles. Just as in natural morality the main elements of "goodness" do not change; so in religious life, spirituality is, amid great varieties of detail, yet, in its leading constituent features, the same thing from one generation to another. But in the life of the individual Christian, or in that of the Church, there is legitimate room for irregular and exceptional forms of activity or excellence. Natural society is not strengthened by the stern repression of all that is peculiar in individual thought or practise; and this is not less true of spiritual or religious society. From the first, high forms of Christian excellence have often been associated with unconscious eccentricity. The eccentricity must be unconscious, because consciousness of eccentricity at once reduces it to a form of vanity which is entirely inconsistent with Christian excellence. How many excellent Christians have been eccentric, deviating more or less from the conventional type of goodness which has been recognized by contemporary religious opinion. They pass away, and when they are gone men do justice to their characters; but while they are still with us how hard do many of us find it to remember that there may be a higher reason for their peculiarities than we think. We know not the full purpose of each saintly life in the designs of Providence; we know not much of the depths and heights whence it draws its inspirations; we can not tell whence it cometh or whither it goeth. Only we know that He whose workmanship it is bloweth where He listeth; and this naturally leads us to remark the practical interpretation which the Holy Spirit often puts upon our Lord's words by selecting as His chosen workmen those who seem to be least fitted by nature for such high service. The apostle has told us how in the first age He set Himself to defeat human anticipations. "Not many wise men after the flesh, not many mighty, not many noble, are called"; learned academies, powerful connections, gentle blood did little enough for the gospel in the days when it won its first and greatest victories. The Holy Spirit, as Nicodemus knew, passed by the varied learning and high station of the Sanhedrin, and breathed where He listed on the peasants of Galilee; He breathed on them a power which would shake the world. And thus has it been again and again in the generations which have followed. When the great Aquinas was a student of philosophy under Albertus Magnus at Cologne, he was known among his contemporaries as "the dumb Ox"; so little did they divine what was to be his place in the theology of Western Christendom. And to those of us who can look back upon the memories of this University for a quarter of a century or more, few things appear more remarkable than the surprizes which the later lives of men constantly afford; sometimes it is a failure of early natural promise, but more often a rich development of intellectual and practical capacity where there had seemed to be no promise at all. We can remember, perhaps, some dull quiet man who seemed to be without a ray of genius, or, stranger still, without anything interesting or marked in character, but who now exerts, and most legitimately, the widest influence for good, and whose name is repeated by thousands with grateful respect. Or we can call to mind another whose whole mind was given to what was frivolous, or even degrading, and who now is a leader in everything that elevates and improves his fellows. The secret of these transfigurations is ever the same. In those days these men did not yet see their way; they were like travelers through the woods at night, when the sky is hidden and all things seem to be other than they are.

Since then the sun has risen and all has changed. The creed of the Church of Christ, in its beauty and its power, has been flashed by the Divine Spirit upon their hearts and understandings; and they are other men. They have seen that there is something worth living for in earnest; that God, the soul, the future, are immense realities, compared with which all else is tame and insignificant. They have learned something of that personal love of our crucified Lord, which is itself a moral and religious force of the highest order, and which has carried them forwards without their knowing it. And what has been will assuredly repeat itself.

141

W. M. TAYLOR

CHRIST BEFORE PILATE—PILATE
BEFORE CHRIST

BIOGRAPHICAL NOTE

WILLIAM MACKERGO TAYLOR, Congregational divine, was born at Kilmarnock, Scotland, in 1829. He was for many years pastor of the Broadway Tabernacle, New York. He had an impressive presence and his delivery was marked by a magnetic earnestness. During the first ten years of his ministry he spoke memoriter, but subsequently wrote out his sermons with detailed care and preached them from manuscript, but their delivery was without the freedom and freshness of extemporaneous address. He came to regret this, for he said: "If I might speak from my own experience I would say, that memoriter preaching is the method which has the greatest advantages, with the fewest disadvantages." He died in 1895.

W. M. TAYLOR

1829—1895

CHRIST BEFORE PILATE—PILATE BEFORE CHRIST [1]

Pilate saith unto them, What shall I do, then, with Jesus, which is called Christ?—Matthew xxvii., 22.

DURING my late visit to my native land I had the great enjoyment of seeing, and somewhat carefully studying, Munkacsy's famous picture of "Christ Before Pilate." Rarely, if ever, had I been so much moved by a work of art; and I propose to give, as nearly as I can recall it, the sermon which it reached to me as I sat silently contemplating the figures, which, even as I looked at them, seemed to grow before me into life.

But, first, I must try to describe to you the picture itself. The canvas is large, and the figures, all of which are on the line of sight, are of life size. The scene is in the pavement or open court before the governor's palace, which was called in the Hebrew tongue Gabbatha, and in which, after all his efforts to

[1] Reprinted by permission from "Contrary Winds and other Sermons," by William M. Taylor, D.D., copyrighted, 1883, by A. C. Armstrong & Son.

wriggle out of the responsibility of dealing
with the case, Pilate ultimately gave up Jesus
to be crucified. At one end of the court, on
a raised bench, and drest in a white toga,
Pilate sits. On either side of him are Jews,
each of whom has a marked and special indi-
viduality. The two on his left are gazing
with intense eagerness at Christ. They are
evidently puzzled, and know not well what
to make of the mysterious prisoner. On his
right, standing on one of the seats, and with
his back against the wall, is a Scribe, whose
countenance is expressive of uttermost contempt, and just in front of this haughty fellow are some Pharisees, one of whom is on his
feet, and passionately urging that Jesus
should be put to death, presumably on the
ground that, if Pilate should let Him go, he
would make it evident that he was not Cæsar's
friend. Before them again is a usurer, sleek,
fat and self-satisfied, clearly taking great comfort to himself in the assurance that, however
the matter may be settled, his well-filled
money-bags will be undisturbed. Beyond him
stands the Christ in a robe of seamless white,
and with His wrists firmly bound; while behind, kept in place by a Roman soldier, standing with his back to the spectator, and making
a barricade with his spear, which he holds
horizontally, is a motley group of onlookers,
not unlike that which we may still see any
day in one of our criminal courts. Of these,

one more furious than the rest is wildly ges-
ticulating, and crying, as we may judge from
his whole attitude, ''Crucify Him! crucify
Him!'' and another, a little to the Savior's
left, but in the second row behind Him, is
leaning forward with mockery in his leering
look, and making almost as if he would spit
upon the saintly one. There is but one really
compassionate face in the crowd, and that is
a face of a woman who, with an infant in her
arms, most fitly represents those gentle daughters of Jerusalem who followed Jesus to Calvary with tears. Then, over the heads of the
on-lookers, and out of the upper part of the
doorway into the court, we get a glimpse of
the quiet light of the morning as it sleeps
upon the walls and turrets of the adjacent
buildings. All these figures are so distinctly
seen that you feel you could recognize them
again if you met them anywhere; and a
strange sense of reality comes upon you as
you look at them, so that you forget that they
are only painted, and imagine that you are
gazing on living and breathing men.

But, as you sit awhile and look on, you
gradually lose all consciousness of the presence
of the mere on-lookers and find your interest
concentrated on these two white-robed ones,
as if they were the only figures before you.
The pose of Christ is admirable. It is repose
blended with dignity; self-possession rising
into majesty. There is no agitation or confu-

sion; no fear or misgiving; but, instead, the calm nobleness of Him who has just been saying, "Thou couldst have no power at all against me, except it were given thee from above; therefore he that delivered me unto thee hath the greater sin." The face alone disappoints. Perhaps that may be owing to the lofty ideal we have of the divine Man, so that no picture of our Lord would entirely please. But tho the painter has wisely abandoned the halo, and all similar conventionalisms of art, and has delineated a real man, for all which he is to be highly commended, yet the eyes which look so steadily at Pilate, as if they were looking him through, seem to me to be cold, keen, and condemnatory, rather than compassionate and sad. It is a conception of the Lord of the same sort as that of Doré, in his well-known picture of the leaving of the Prætorium, and the eyes have not in them that deep well of tenderness out of which came the tears which He shed over Jerusalem, and which we expect to see in them when He is looking at the hopeless struggle of a soul which will not accept His aid. It is said that the artist, dissatisfied with his first attempt, has painted the Christ face twice; but this, also, is a partial failure, and here, so at least it seemed to me as I looked upon it, is the one defect in his noble work. But if there is this defect, it is one which it shares with every other effort that human art has made

to delineate the Lord. The Pilate, however,
is well-nigh faultless. Here is a great, strong
man, the representative of the mightiest empire the world has ever seen, with a head
indicating intellectual force, and a face, especially in its lower part, suggestive of sen-
sual indulgence. There is ordinarily no want
of firmness in him, as we may see from the
general set of his features; but now there is
in his countenance a marvelous mixture of
humiliation and irresolution. He cannot lift
his eyes to meet the gaze of Christ; and while
one of his hands is nervously clutching at
his robe he is looking sadly into the other,
whose fingers, even as we look at them, almost
seem to twitch with perplexed irresolution.
He is clearly pondering for himself the question which a few moments before he had ad-
drest to the multitude, "What shall I do
with Jesus which is called Christ?" He is
annoyed that the case has been brought to
him at all, and as he feels himself drifting
on, against his own better judgment, toward
yielding to the clamor of the multitude, he
falls mightily in his own conceit, and begins
to despise himself. He would, at that moment, give, oh, how much! to be rid of the
responsibility of dealing with the Christ, but
he cannot evade it; and so he sits there, drifting on to what he knows is a wrong decision,
the very incarnation of the feeling which his
own national poet described when he said, "I

see and approve the better course; I follow the worse." Thus, as we look at these two, we begin to discover that it was not Christ that was before Pilate so much as Pilate was before Christ. His was the testing experience. His was the trial; his too, alas! was the degradation; and at that coming day when the places shall be reversed, when Christ shall be on the judgment seat, and Pilate at the bar, there will still be that deep self-condemnation which the painter here has fixt upon his countenance. It is a marvelous picture, in many respects the most remarkable I ever looked upon, and, even from this imperfect description of it, you will easily understand how, as I sat intent before it, it stirred my soul to the very depths.

But now, with this portrayal of the scene before us let us see if we can account, first, for the hesitation of Pilate to give up the Lord, and then for his final yielding to the clamor of the people. Why all this reluctance on his part to send Jesus to the cross? He was not usually so scrupulous. A human life more or less gave him generally very little concern. He had all a Roman's indifference for the comfort of those who stood in any respect in his way; and had no compunction, as we know, in mingling the blood of certain turbulent Jews with the very sacrifices which at the moment they were offering. Had Christ been a Roman citizen, indeed, he would most likely have been very watchful over His safety, for in regard to all such the imperial law was peculiarly strict, but the life of a mere Jew was a very small thing in his estimation. Wherefore, then, this unwonted squeamishness of conscience? It was the result of a combination of particulars, each of which had a special force of its own, and the aggregate of which so wrought upon his mind that he was brought thereby to a stand.

There was, in the first place, the peculiar character of the prisoner. A very slight examination had been sufficient to convince him that Christ was innocent of the charge which had been brought against Him. But in the course of that examination much more than the innocence of Christ had come to view. He had manifested a dignified patience altogether unlike anything that Pilate had ever seen; and His answers to certain questions had been so strangely suggestive of something higher and nobler than even the most exalted earthly philosophy that he could not look upon Him as a common prisoner. He was no mere fanatic; neither was He after the pattern of any existing school, whether Jewish, Greek, or Roman. There was about Him an "other-worldliness" which brought those near Him into close proximity, for the time, with the unseen; and an elevation which lifted Him above the tumult that was howling for His destruction. Probably Pilate could not

have described it to himself, but there was
something which he felt unusual and exceptional in this man, marking Him out from
every other he ever had before him, and con-
straining him to take a special interest in
His case. Add to this that his wife had sent
to him that singular message—"Have thou
nothing to do with that just man, for I have
suffered many things this day in a dream
because of him,"—a message which, in those
days of mingled scepticism and superstition
—for the two always go hand in hand—must
have produced a deep impression on his mind.
Moreover, there seemed some fatality about
the case. He had tried to roll it over upon
Herod, but that wily monarch sent the prisoner back upon his hands. He had attempted
to release Him, as the Passover prisoner for
the year, but neither was there any outlet for
him in that, for the people had preferred
Barabbas. And so the responsibility had come
again to his own door, and could not be passed
on to another. Still again, he saw that the
Jews were acting most hypocritically in the
matter. It was a new thing for them to be
zealous for the honor of Cæsar, and he could
easily see through the mask they wore into
the envy and malice which were the motives
for their conduct. The deeper he went into
the case he discovered only the more reason
for resisting their importunity, and, however,
he looked at it, his plain duty was to set the
prisoner free.

Why then, again we ask, was his perplexity? The answer is suggested by the taunt of the Jews, "If thou let this man go thou art not Cæsar's friend; whosoever maketh himself a king speaketh against Cæsar." He foresaw that if he resisted the will of the rulers he would make them his enemies, and so provoke them to complain of him to the emperor, who would then institute an inquiry into the administration of his office—and that he was not prepared to face. He had done things as a governor which would not bear the light, and so at the crisis of his life he was fettered by deeds of the past from doing that which he felt to be the duty of the present. You may, perhaps, remember that expression of the prophet, which thus reads in the margin: "Their doings will not suffer them to turn unto their God": and that other, which affirms, concerning Israel: "Their own doings have beset them about." Now these descriptions most accurately define the cause of Pilate's perplexity here. His conduct in the past had been such that he had not the courage to take any course which might lead to an investigation of that. If he could deliver Christ without provoking that, then he would most cheerfully do so; but if by delivering Christ he would provoke that, then Christ must be given up to the cross. Hence his perplexity at the first, and hence, also, his yielding in the end. His past misdeeds had put him virtually into the power of those who were now so eager for the condemnation of the Christ. On three several occasions his arbitrariness had been such as all but to instigate a rebellion among the people, and his cruelty and contempt for justice, when he had a personal end to gain, were sure, upon appeal to the emperor, to be severely punished; so to save himself from banishment and disgrace, if not even death, he delivered over Jesus to the will of the Jews. He wished to do right in this case more than ever he had wished before; there was something about it which in his view made it more important that he should do right now than ever before; but through all his past official life he had, by his enormities and oppressions, been unconsciously weaving round himself a net, in the meshes of which he was now inextricably caught. His guilty conscience made him a coward at the very time when most of all he wanted to be brave. He had come to his "narrow place," where he could turn neither to the right hand nor to the left, but must face the naked alternative "yes" or "no"; and he fell because in his former life, when he was thinking of no such ordeal, he had sold himself by his evil deeds into the power of the enemy.

Now, what a lesson there is in all this for us! Men think that they may live for the time being as they please, and that at a convenient season they can repent and turn to God. But the present is conditioning the future, and making it either possible or the reverse for us to do right in the future. He who neglects the laws of health every day, and lives in intemperance and excess of all kinds, is only making it absolutely certain that when fever lays him low he will die, for he has eaten out the strength of his constitution by his follies. And, in the same way, he who sets all morality at defiance in his ordinary conduct only makes it inevitable that when his convenient season does come, when his time of privilege and testing does arrive, he will fail to rise to the occasion, and be swept away into perdition. The tenor of our ordinary life determines how we shall pass through exceptional and crucial occasions, therefore let us bring that up to the highest level by doing everything as unto God, and then we shall be ready for any emergency.

Nor let me forget to add here, that in spite of all his efforts to keep back investigation, Pilate's day of reckoning with the emperor did come. The Jews complained of him after all, in spite of his yielding to them now; and as the result he was banished, and afterwards, so tradition says, he committed suicide. Thus the ordeal and the disgrace came, notwithstanding all he did to avert them, and he had not under them the solace which he might have enjoyed if only he had stood firm on this great and memorable occasion. Therefore let us all, and especially the young, take to ourselves, as the first lesson from this deeply interesting history, that we should be careful not to hamper ourselves for the discharge of duty in the future by guilt of the present. By our conduct now we are either coiling cords around us which shall hold us fast at the very time when we most desire to be free, or we are forming and fostering a strength of character which, through God, will triumph over every temptation. If "to be weak is to be miserable," it is no less true that to be guilty is to be weak. Preserve yourselves, therefore, from this danger, and seek above all other things to keep your consciences clean; then when you will need all your strength for a crisis, you will not sit, like Pilate here, in nervous perplexity bemoaning your helplessness even while you yield to the adversary; but you will shake the temptation from you with as much ease as the eagle shakes the dewdrop from his wing. Keep yourselves pure: so shall your youth be full of happiness, and you shall go forth out of it with no encumbering past to clog the wheels of your endeavor. How happy he whose youth thus leaves him with a smile and sends him forth upon the duties of manhood with a benediction! But he, how miserable! whose early years heap bitter maledictions on his head, and push him forward into active life with a conscience already laden with guilt, and a soul as weak before temptation as a reed is before the wind.

But while there is thus in this history a lesson for all time, I think Munkacsy, by the appearance of his wondrous picture now, has made it evident that there is also something in it specially adapted to these modern days. It is with artists in the choice of their subjects as it is with ministers in the selection of their themes. Both alike, consciously and unconsciously, and most frequently perhaps unconsciously, are affected by the spirit of their age. The atmosphere—literary, moral, political, and religious—which is round about them, and which they are daily breathing, does, insensibly to themselves, so influence them that their thoughts are turned by it into a channel different from that in which those of a former generation flowed. Hence, whether the painter would admit it or not, I see in this picture, at this juncture, at once a mirror of the times and a lesson for them. The question of Pilate, "What shall I do, then, with Jesus which is called the Christ?" is preeminently the question of the present age. No doubt we may say with truth that it has been the question of all the Christian centuries, and each one of them has faced it and solved it after its own fashion. It has tested the centuries even as it tested Pilate, and those in which Christ was rejected have been the darkest in the world's history; while those in which He has been hailed as the incarnate God have been the brightest which the earth has ever seen, because irradiated with truth, and justice, and benevolence and purity. But tho we are always prone to exaggerate that in the midst of which we are ourselves, it seems to me that in no one age since that of the primitive Church has this jesting question been so prominent as in our own. All the controversies of our times, social, philosophical, and theological, lead up to and find their ultimate hinge in the answer to this inquiry, "Who is this Jesus Christ?" If He be a mere man, then there is for us nothing but uncertainty on any subject, outside of the domain of the exact sciences; and we must all become agnostics, holding this one negative article of belief, that nothing can be known about anything save that of which we can take cognizance with the bodily sense. But if He be incarnate God, then He brings with Him from heaven the final word on all subjects concerning which He has spoken; and tho in His person He is the mystery of mysteries, yet, at once received, He becomes forthwith the solution of all mysteries, and faith in Him is at once the satisfaction of the intellect and the repose of the heart. It is perfectly natural, therefore, that all the controversies of the day should turn on Him. The lives of Christ which have been written during the last thirty or forty years would make in themselves a very respectable library; and the cry even of the sceptic is, "I could get on very well with unbelief, if I only knew what to make of Christ." Yes, that is just the difficulty. Christ is here in the Scriptures a character portrayed in literature; He was in the world for thirty-three years, and lived a life exceptional in every respect, but most of all in the moral and spiritual departments, so that of Him alone perfection can be predicated; He has been ever since a most potent factor in history, for through His influence all that is pure, and noble, and exalted, and lovely and of good report, has come into our civilization. Now, these things have to be accounted for. If He was only a man, how shall we explain them? And if He was more than a man shall we not take His own testimony as to His dignity and mission? If we are to be unbelievers, we must account for Christ on natural principles; but if we cannot do that, then we must conceive Him as He claims to be conceived. There is no alternative. Those in the age who have the spirit and dispositon of Pilate will anew reject Him! but those who are sincere and earnest in their inquiries will come ultimately out into the light, for "if any man be willing to do his will, he shall know of the doctrine whether it be of God."

And what is true of the age, as a whole, is true also of every individual to whom the gospel is proclaimed. For each of us, my hearers, this is the question of questions, "What shall I do with Jesus which is called Christ?" Shall I reject Him and live precisely as if I had never heard His name? or shall I accept Him as the Lord from heaven in human nature, trust in Him as my Savior, and obey Him as my King? I must do the one or the other; and yet how many are seeking, like Pilate, to evade the question? They try to escape the responsibility of dealing with it as a direct alternative of yes or no. But as one has well said, "necessity is laid upon us. The adversaries of Christ press upon us to give our verdict against Him. We are troubled and perplexed, for we have long heard about Him, and have had each of us his own convictions. We would still remain neutral. We try—and try in vain—to escape from the spirit, the conversation, the literature, the question of the times. Again and again we wash our hands. But neither our silence nor our actions are of any avail; and so we are found sitting, conscious of the presence and the claims of our Savior, and, like Pilate, not daring to look at Him, as we puzzle over the answer which we must give to the question that is being forced upon us—Who is this Jesus Christ?" Perhaps this description accurately portrays some one here this morning.

If so, let me give him one parting word.

It is this: You can not evade the decision, but be sure that you look at the Christ before you give Him up. Nothing is so remarkable in the picture to which I have so often this day referred as the evident persistency with which Pilate keeps his eyes from Christ; and few things are so saddening as to meet with men who profess to have, and really have, difficulties about Christ, but who have never read the gospels or the New Testament with any attention.

Let me urge you earnestly, therefore, to study these gospels and epistles before you give your voice against the Lord, and I am very sure that if you ponder them thoroughly you will soon accept Him. Give over trying to solve all the difficulties and so-called discrepancies in the Scriptures which form the stock-in-trade of the infidel lecturer—all these are but as dust which he raises that he may blind your eyes to the really important question, "Who is Christ?" Settle that, and if you do, all other difficulties will vanish. Turn your face to the light, and the shadow will fall behind you. Look at the Christ before you give Him up. And remember, if you do reject Christ, you have still to account for Him. It is unreasonable for you, if you believe only in the natural and material, to leave such a phenomenon as Christ unexplained.

Yes, and I must add here that if you reject

Him you must yet account to Him. Go, then, and ponder this text; yea, may it continue sounding in your inmost heart until you have determined to receive and rest upon Him as your only Savior, and say to Him, like Thomas, "My Lord and my God."

JOHN HALL

LIBERTY ONLY IN TRUTH

BIOGRAPHICAL NOTE

JOHN HALL was born at Market Hill, County Armagh, Ireland, in 1829. For many years he was pastor of the Fifth Avenue Presbyterian Church, New York, where he had a large and devoted following. He was of fine physique, and there was a power in face and voice that at once commanded his audience. He spoke without manuscript, and his style was marked by great sincerity, directness and earnestness. He died in 1899.

JOHN HALL

1829—1899

LIBERTY ONLY IN TRUTH

And I will walk at liberty, for I seek thy precepts.—
Psalms cxix., 45.

GOD is the Governor of this world. Some one may say, that is a very elementary truth. Even so; there have been long ages in the history of our race when that truth was not accepted and when the most intelligent of our race believed something directly opposed. There have been multitudes of men, for example, who believed, like Aristotle, that matter is eternal. There are multitudes still who believe that in some way or other nature governs itself. There is a large class of thinkers who, without taking the name to themselves, are practically pantheists, and, like Spinoza and Fichte and Hegel, persuade themselves that all is God, as they express it, and that God is all. You do not need to be told that the earlier portion of the Old Testament Scriptures God has given to us that we might have these illusions banished, and that we might be made to know that God is the Creator and the Ruler of all things, that He is not nature, and nature is not God; that He is not to be confounded with the works of His hands; that He is a distinct, personal and holy Being, who has created all, and who has a right, on the ground of creation, even if there were no other, to be the Ruler of all. It took long to make men understand this truth, simple and elementary as it seems to you and to me.

When we say that God governs the globe, we do not mean the mere earthly, solid structure on which we dwell. We mean that He governs the inhabitants of it, the communities and the individuals. "The Lord reigneth, let the earth rejoice." "The Lord reigneth, let the nations tremble." "He raiseth up kings and he putteth them down." He calls into being Pharaohs that He may show His power and His glory in relation to them. His providence is most holy and wise and powerful, and it is not general merely, it is particular, extending to all the creatures and to all their actions. These things we have to keep in mind in relation to Jehovah.

Now it would seem, surely, that if a man believed this his common sense would dictate to him that, living in a world that God had made and God rules in every detail, if he wishes to be happy in it, he must have respect to the law of Him who has made and who rules. Common sense indicates that if we live in a house it is desirable to be on good terms with the head of the house if we wish to be comfortable. Common sense dictates that if a man is in the employment of others, it is wise for him to have a right understanding, to stand well with the head of the department in which he is engaged. Common sense teaches us that if we are subjects in a kingdom and wish to be safe and happy, we must respect the laws by which the kingdom is ruled. And we have only to extend this principle, and we get to the point that was before the Psalmist's mind when he says: "I will walk at liberty, for I seek (or, as it is in the revision, without changing the meaning, 'I have sought') thy statutes." I am living in Thy world, I am dependent upon Thee, I have taken pains to know what Thy will is, that I may do it; and so I walk at liberty. That is the idea that is brought to us in the text, and it is easy for you to see how good and practical that idea is.

But the question may arise, can we know the precepts and the statutes that God has given to us? You do not need to be told that that is within our reach. God has spoken to us in this revelation, as He did speak less articulately in the works of His hands, and in the instincts and convictions that He produced in our spirit. We have His revelation in our hands. We can seek the knowledge of it. In many instances well-meaning and right-minded boys, under great difficulties, have sought education that they may get on in this world. In many other cases boys have had education at their very doors, and have never sought it, and consequently have been of little account in the world. Now the difference is not great, in this aspect of it, between ordinary secular education and the spiritual education of which the text gives us an illustration. Here are God's statutes and precepts put within our reach. We can search them, seek them, know them and do them, by the grace that God is willing to give, or we can push them aside, ignore and disregard them, and take our own way, and the result will be absolute and everlasting failure in our lives. We can not have this too solemnly fixt in our thoughts. God has spoken to us. What shall we do with His word? Shall we neglect it and pass it by, or shall we take it, study it, seek it, as the verse expresses it, and make it the rule of our lives? Jesus Christ has come down from heaven to live among us, and has said to our race, "Come unto me and learn of me"; and there are millions to whom this message has come and they disregard and ignore it; they do not come to Him, they do not learn of Him. Can we wonder if the Judge should say to them when they appear at His seat, "I never knew you"? If you read the First Epistle to the Thessalonians, you will see pictures of an angry God, as an avenging fire, in the apostle's description. On whom does the fire fall? On whom does the Judge show his indignation? Is it upon the misers and the miscreants and the murderers of the race merely? Oh, no. It is upon them that "know not God and obey not the gospel of his Son." Is it any wonder that the sacred writer should say, "Remember thy Creator in the days of thy youth"; not merely remember that there is a God—remember thy Creator, who made thee and in whose hand thy fortunes are. Remember in the days of thy youth, the formative days, the days when character is being shaped. What is well begun is half ended. The life that is well begun in this way has a guaranty of usefulness and success. The life that is not begun in this way has a dark and gloomy prospect before it. Remember thy Creator. We all know well what is meant when some one says to us, on going away from our homes, "Don't forget your home, don't forget your mother." We know what that means. And God's messenger speaks to us in the same tone when he makes this appeal: Remember thy Creator; remember His power, remember His will, remember His statutes, seek His precepts, and by doing this thou wilt be able to walk at liberty.

You may have mere liberty, and not light and not the liberty of God. You may combine liberty with means, with power, and with a certain degree of prosperity; you may combine it with equality and with fraternity, and yet not have the true enlightenment. True enlightenment comes in the way, indicated in the text, by the seeking of God's precepts, the knowing of God's statutes, and this you and I need to keep in mind. "What is liberty?" once asked Burke. "What is liberty without wisdom and without virtue? Such liberty is the greatest of all possible evils, for it is vice and folly and madness, without tuition and without restraint." Mere liberty without other forces working in the sphere that it opens up, is only another name for license. "Give me liberty or give me death," said Patrick Henry —not because he felt the need of enlightenment. He had been enlightened by the teaching of an intelligent Scottish father, by the preaching of the splendid sermons of Samuel Davies, and especially by the daily study, which he kept up to his dying day, of his Bible. He had been enlightened by these things. What he craved for himself and for his fellow men was open space in which, unhindered, other and mighty influences might tell upon his fellow men and make the country what, in the blessing of God, it has become. Settle this in your minds: Liberty is simply the freedom for other forces to act, and it is for you and me who are free, to see what these forces are, and we never can have any so good as those which the Psalmist speaks of when he says that he sought God's precepts, he studied God's statutes, that he might do them, and so walk at liberty. We want to walk at liberty.

How can we do it? If we do not thus walk at liberty, there is only one alternative—stay in bondage and walk in bondage, moving about indeed, and apparently free, but with moral chains binding our natures and our whole being in bondage to the powers that will rejoice in our misery and ultimate ruin. It is to make men understand this that we have such institutions as we enjoy to-day. For this end church edifices are reared. For this end people are invited to come and be regularly in them and under their influence. For this end God has been pleased to give us the day of holy rest. For this purpose the ministry has been instituted. Our business is to make men seek and know God's precepts and statutes, that they may do them and that they may walk at liberty. We ministers are for you; our business is to seek your moral and spiritual good, your full and complete liberation. Our business is to enlighten you with the truth as God has been pleased to reveal it unto us. You do not come to these churches for our sakes, to hear us. You do not give your money that we may be sustained and upheld. I tell you I would rather sweep the streets, I would rather carry bricks on my shoulder to the builder, than be a mere official person maintained because he can teach so much and get so many people to hear him. Brethren, it is that you may be enlightened and saved with the light of life, that God has brought us into the position in which we are now together. Keep this in your thoughts; and that you may be enlightened and free, look upward and not downward, nor around you. In that statue in our harbor, the light that will shine is light that comes, I suppose, from the heart of the earth; but the light that is to enlighten the world is the light of the sun, the Sun of Righteousness. See that you have that shining into your souls, that you may walk at liberty.

Having looked at the former part of this text, namely, what the Psalmist did with a view to the end, we look at the end at which he was aiming. He studied God's Word, not simply that he might have so much intellectual knowledge. He studied it for practical uses. He studied God's precepts that he might obey them. I do not need to remind you that you and I have advantages greater than he had, in some important respects. He had the revelation in part; we have it in its completeness. He had the preparatory dispensation; we have the dispensation that fulfils the promises of the preparatory. He had the beginning; we have the complement. We know more than he did. He wrote these words, "I have sought thy precepts." He knew of the Paschal Lamb and of its typical significance; we know the Lamb of God that taketh away the sin of the world. He knew the Hebrew priest and the

general character of his functions. We know
a High Priest who has passed into the heavens,
Jesus, the Son of God. He knew of the altar
and the victim, and the blood that made typical atonement; we know of the great sacrifice
on the cross, bringing in a redemption that is
complete and eternal. He knew of a Messiah
that was to come. You, even children in the
Sunday-school to-day, know of that Messiah
risen, risen triumphant, risen a conqueror,
risen for you, risen because He has finished
the work God gave Him to do. If the Psalmist
studied God's will that he might walk at liberty, how much greater is the obligation upon
us to do the same, and how much greater our
facilities and our encouragement. Let us try,
then, to travel in the Psalmist's steps, and
let us see some, not all, of the forms of liberty
that we can have by compliance with the
divine precepts.

There is liberty, in the first place, from the
world. I use the word now in the sense in
which it is used so frequently in the Bible—
not merely this round globe or the hundreds
of millions that are upon it—not merely these
millions in that capacity. The world lieth in
the wicked one; the mass of men, that is, do
not know God. They constitute the world of
the New Testament; we can be in bondage to
this world. Natural men are in bondage to
it. They are not at liberty in relation to
that natural world. It is without God; it does

173

not ask what His will is. It enquires as to
its own will, and it tries to enforce it. You
sometimes see cliques and coteries and collec-
tions of men insisting at any cost upon carrying out their own will. This is only the spirit
of the greater world of which they constitute
a section. Sometimes men are in bondage
to the world in this sense, and the mainspring
of their life is to stand well with it, to do what
their set, their society, the world round about
them, wishes them to do. Sometimes the bondage is aggravated by another feature, viz.,
the effort to rise higher, to get upon a more
elevated plane, to get into another set; and,
oh, how aggravated is the bondage under
which many thus live and labor! Freedom
from that is obtained when we walk according
to God's statutes. Believers, the world is not
your master. One is your Master, even Christ,
and we are brethren in Him, and He is reason-
able and kind and just and brotherly, and you
can walk with Him. His favor is enough for
you, His smile satisfies you. Fellowship with
Him is the best society. Let society stigmatize
you, let it stamp its enmity upon you, but
seek God's precepts. If you only have Christ
walking with you, then you walk at liberty.
But as to the life-work in which many are
busy, or trying to get up a little higher so-
cially, take this precept of the Word, "Godliness with contentment is great gain"; and
these things, the godliness with the content-

ment, will break these clanking chains of insane and stupid ambition and will prepare you to walk at liberty. "I am in the place where God puts me. I am trying to do the work that God gives to me. I am responsible to Him. I belong to Him. He is my Father, Christ is my Brother, heaven is my home. This I believe on the authority of His word. I will walk at liberty." Let me commend that form of true freedom to you.

There is liberty, in the second place, from bad ways. Do I need to describe these bad ways to you? You can not live in the city, you can not read the newspapers, you can not hear the gossip, you can not know what is going on in the circles in which you mingle, without knowing some of these bad ways. There is the lover of this world's possessions, so strongly denounced in Isaiah's prophecies: beginning, perhaps, with necessary saving, but coming slowly but steadily to a sordid love of the thing that is saved, till the whole spirit is mercenary, and gold is the deity that is practically worshiped. There is the drunkard, sipping a little innocently, as he thinks, at the beginning, then going a little farther, and secretly, until shame is lost and the victim is under the power of the drink—degraded, wretched, irresponsible, not ashamed of himself, for shame is gone, but an object for which all are ashamed that are connected with him. There is the gambler, beginning perhaps with what he deemed innocent recreation, and catching the spirit of the thing till it masters him, until he flings away all that he has, and all that he hopes to have, in the chance of recovering something already lost, till life is a burden and fortune is gone, and suicide is perhaps the tragical termination. These are specimens of the bad ways—marked specimens, I grant, but still simple specimens. There is freedom from this when we seek and do God's statutes—real freedom. We learn to walk circumspectly; we learn to keep the heart with all diligence; we learn to hate evil and to do good; we learn to flee from the snares that Satan sets for the feet of men. We walk securely, for we have been taught of the Spirit to walk with God. Make sure, dear hearers, that you have this liberty.

There is liberty from bad memories—bad, putrid memories. When the corrupt imagination contemplates indulgences in sin, it often dwells upon these long before the actual execution of them, and as they linger in the mind they photograph themselves upon its surface, and they stay there. There may be compunction for the sin, there may be shame over it, there may be vows against it, there may be honest purposes to resist and overcome it, and these purposes to a good degree carried out; but the horrid, poisonous memories remain in the soul. You know what it is to be in a house where

animal matter is decaying and poisoning
fumes are being scattered up and down. Oh!
the misery of the human mind that is haunted
with the ghosts of bad deeds that have been
done in the past. It is bondage of the keenest
and sorest kind. There is liberty from these
to those who walk in God's statutes, liberty
that can be had nowhere else. "A new heart
will I give you, and a right spirit will I put
within you. I will take away the stony heart
out of your flesh, and I will give you a heart
of flesh." Happy are they to whom this
word was fulfilled in their early youth, and
who in consequence were kept from the sins,
the very recollection of which is sometimes
like the beginning of hell.

There is bondage to bad associates and bad
associations. In how many instances, in
thoughtlessness, inexperience, under the impulses of mere feeling, do men become en-
tangled in connections that mar their lives
and spoil all their happiness—make happiness practically impossible! I speak what
I know, when I say that there are too many
cases in which boys are practically ruined
where they go as pupils to schools away
from their parents' supervision, thrown into
dependence, in some degree, upon those whom
they call friends, and these friends bad, ini-
tiating them into ways and habits and
modes of thinking and doing, for which they
only want the liberty of later years that they

may put them into practise, with disgrace,
misery and ruin. Relief from this bondage,
escape from it, these can be had when we seek
God's statutes, when we walk according to His
precepts. Wisdom's ways are pleasantness,
and her paths are peace. There are no bad
habits in them; there are no entangling associations in them; there are no corrupting and
degrading influences in them. There is
nothing in them that plays upon passion, till
passion, once our idol and our sport, becomes
our ruler and our cruel tyrant. To escape all
these, this is the way: seek God's statutes, that
you may know and do them, and you shall
walk at liberty.

BACON

GOD INDWELLING

BIOGRAPHICAL NOTE

LEONARD WOOLSEY BACON, Congregational divine, born in New Haven, Conn., 1830. He was educated at Yale, from which university he graduated in 1850. He has filled the position of pastor in many important churches and has done much theological and literary work. Among other things he edited Luther's "Deutsche Geistliche Lieder" (New York, 1883), and wrote "History of American Christianity" (New York, 1897).

BACON

Born in 1830

GOD INDWELLING [1]

Thus saith the high and lofty One that inhabiteth eternity, whose name is Holy: I dwell in the high and holy place, with him also that is of a contrite and humble spirit, to revive the spirit of the humble, and to revive the heart of the contrite ones.—Isaiah lvii., 15.

INHABITING eternity; yet making His abode within a broken heart! It seems as if we might apprehend either of these things singly; but both together—how can it be? The distresses, the wants, the fears, of life, make us long that indeed it were so. Our soul crieth out for God, for the living God.

We cry; but there seems no answer; only an awful silence. We look upon the outward facts of life and death, and see the steady, unswerving march of law—the unbroken, irrefragable chain of causes and effects—never yielding nor bending to all our needs, to all our prayers. And God seems so far, so far away! We turn the pages of our knowledge from the physical to the metaphysical, and

---

[1] From "The Simplicity That Is in Christ," published by Funk & Wagnalls Company.

we come no nearer. Our philosophical, our theological, yes, our religious meditations upon the nature and attributes of the infinite One—the omniscient, the eternal, the unchangeable—set Him more and more beyond the reach of our fellowship and prayer. But all the time, one thing testifies to us of a heavenly Father that hears and loves and answers, and that is our ineradicable need. The cravings of our nature cannot be rebuked by scientific observation of the constancy of law, nor by philosophic meditation of the properties of absolute and infinite being. We need, we must have, a Father. Our heart and flesh, our soul, crieth out for the living God.

In such a strait, there is true comfort in this word of the Lord by His prophet, in which the full measure of the difficulty is set forth, and the solution of it is found in faith.

It has seemed to me that we need not seek in vain in the created works of God for helps to that faith by which we know that the infinite and eternal God can have fellowship with us and can dwell within the narrow precincts of a human heart.

That sight in visible nature which gives to us the highest sense of vastness,—the aptest suggestion of infinity,—is doubtless the aspect of the starry heavens;—to all of us, ignorant or learned, poetic or unimaginative. It needs no diagrams nor distances from a book of astronomy to tell the lessons of the firmament.

"Their sound is gone out into all the earth, and their words to the end of the world."

And yet it is when we come to study the dimensions of this operation in detail, that the sense of its vastness grows upon us and overpowers us. David never could have felt, as we can feel, the force of his own words:

When I consider thy heavens, the work of thy fingers,
The moon and the stars which thou hast ordained,
What is man that thou art mindful of him,
And the sun of man that thou visitest him!

They are like the chariot of Ezekiel's vision, "so high that it was dreadful." It seems a fearful thing to have to do with such magnitudes; and when we hear of scholars in their observatories measuring the distances among the stars, it overcomes us with a giddy feeling, as when we see men clambering on church spires, or crossing the East River on a strand of wire. A row of figures on a slate does seem such a frail support on which to go marching through the starry spaces! We almost shudder when we see human science springing clear of the narrow boundaries of the earth, and on such attenuated threads of calculation venturing boldly forth to other planets, and thence over chasms of space so vast that it is easiest to call them infinite, until he reaches the fixt stars. No longer content with numbering and naming the host of heaven, and marshaling them in constellations, this tiny

creature must take upon himself to scrutinize
their constitution, must weigh their floating
bulk, must

> "Speed his flight from star to star,
>   From world to luminous world, as far
>   As the universe rears his flaming wall,"

and, as if bearing in this amazing flight the
measuring-rod which once the prophet saw in
an angel's hand, must measure the paths
along which the planets travel, and tell in
human language the distances on the chart
of heaven.

And how human language staggers under
the burden thus laid upon it! We begin with
attempting to state the least of these distances
in numbers of a unit of earthly distance, but,
when we speak of some of our near neighbors
in celestial space as being twenty trillions of
English miles away, the words will not hold
the meaning—they carry no conception to the
mind. They are good to cipher with, but that
is all they are good for. We try to invent a
new form of speech, and for our unit we take
the distance which a cannon-ball, if retaining
the velocity with which it leaves the gun,
would travel in twenty-four hours, and say
that, at this rate of speed, it would take so
many months, and years, and centuries, to
reach such and such of the nearer stars. But
this, too, is a clumsy failure; and we resort,
at last, to the heavens themselves for a stan-

dard of measurement, and find it in the velocity of light. It shoots from the sun to the
earth, a distance of ninety-two millions of
miles, in eight minutes and seven seconds.
And we attempt to represent the distance of
certain of the stars by stating how many
years, how many hundred years, how many
thousand years, it takes a ray of their light
to reach the earth. But it is all in vain. We
commonly speak of imagination as outstrip-
ping, in its speed, the slow-paced reason; but
here it is the reason that has outrun the
imagination. From these unspeakable tracts
of space, over which the reason of man has
not hesitated to go,

"Sounding along its dim and perilous way,"

the imagination shrinks back and refuses to
follow. We know things which we cannot
conceive. In presence of such stupendous
magnitudes,

"Imagination's utmost stretch
In wonder dies away."

We can only bow with awe in the presence
of things which the calmest computations have
revealed, and seizing the words kindled on
the lips of inspiration, sing aloud in worship:

"O Lord, how great are thy works!
In wisdom hast thou made them all!"

I have shown you what is wonderful. Come
now and I will show you what is more won-

derful. For I will show you these infinite
spaces of the sky, and the glory of them, and
the innumerable host of starry worlds, gathered up in a moment of time, within the tiny
pupil of a human eye. It is wonderful that
the heavens and the host of them should be
so great; but that, being so great, they should
be able to become so infinitely little,—this
passes all wonder. The shepherd stretched
upon the ground amid his sheep gazes up into
the starry depths, and finds them wonderful;
but never thinks how far more wonderful than
the heavens which he beholds is himself beholding them. As he lies gazing, long lines
of light, from planet and star and constella-
tion, come stretching on through the infinite
void spaces, to center on the lenses of his
drowsy eye. Side by side, and all at once,
yet never twisted or confused, these ten thousand rays of different light enter the little
aperture in the center of the eye which we
call the pupil. There they cross, in a point
which has no dimensions, and separate again,
and paint in microscopic miniature upon the
little surface of the retina, behind the eye-
ball, the inverted facsimile of the visible heavens. There, in the ante-chamber of the brain,
marches Orion, with his shining baldric and
his jeweled sword; there glow Arcturus and
Sirius, and the steadfast North Star; there
pass the planets to and fro; and the far-off
nebulæ are painted there with suffused and

gentle radiance—all the heavens and the glory of them gathered in that slender filament of light, threaded through that tiny aperture, painted by their own rays upon that little patch of nervous network, apprehended, felt, known through and through by that finite human mind. How far stranger and sublimer a thing is this than the mere bulk of the worlds, or the mere chasms of void space in which they hang weltering!

By this sublime fact of God's visible creation, we are led on to apprehend and feel the sublimest of the glories of God Himself, set forth in the prophet's words,—that He whose lifetime is infinite duration, whose dwelling-place is infinite space,—He who before the earth and the world were made was no younger, neither will be older when they are all consumed,—whose presence reaches out to the farthest fixt star that eye or telescope has ever described floating upon the far verge of the universe, and occupies beyond in all the orbits of worlds yet undiscovered, and still beyond in the regions of space where is naught but the possibility of future worlds, and fills all this immensity to repletion,— that this "high and lofty One that inhabiteth eternity" should enter into some poor, crusht and broken spirit, that trembles at the very whisper of His voice, and should make the narrow recesses of that heart His abode, His home. This is the mystery and glory of the

Godhead,—not alone that He should be infinite, eternal, immortal, invisible, but that being all these, He should yet be apprehended by the little mind of a man, and call Himself that man's Friend and Comforter and Father.

For it is not more evident that the tiny pupil of human eye can take in the expanses and abysses of the heavens, than it is that the little soul of man can receive into itself the infinite God.

I. Man receives God into himself by the intellect. We trifle with the facts of our own consciousness, if we suffer the theological description of God as incomprehensible to divert us from the fact that our minds are made for nothing more expressly than for this, that they should receive God. The lowest rudiments of the knowledge of the simplest forms of matter are the beginnings of the knowledge of God. If we could remember, you and I, now that we are grown, all that came to us in infancy—the first struggles of the childish mind with the questions that we are not done with yet, we should see how soon the knowledge of God comes to the little one. Beyond the cradle in which it wakes up to the wonders of a new day is the nursery, and beyond the nursery is the house, and beyond the house is the garden, and beyond the garden there lies all the world, and beyond the world shuts down the sky with its stars, and beyond the sky—what? "Tell me, father—tell me, mother, what is there beyond the sky?'' And, according to your knowledge or your ignorance, your faith or your unbelief, you may tell the little questioner of heaven, or of infinities of other worlds, or of infinite waste room and empty space, and he will believe you. But attempt to tell him that beyond is nothing, and not even room for anything, and will he believe you? He may seem to believe you, but it is impossible that he really should believe. The infant mind—any mind —rejects it as impossible. It cannot live in anything less than infinite space. It stifles. It leaps up and beats its wings against any bars with which you would cage it in, but that it will break through and take possession of its inheritance.

And as with infinite extent, so with infinite duration. How well I remember, as a very little child, when men were talking of the end of the world, and the great comet stretched amain across the sky, and men's hearts were failing them for fear, how the thought of infinite duration prest in, inexorably, on my soul! Come judgment day, come final conflagration, come end of all material things, come cessation and extinction of all angels, all souls, all sentient creatures, still this could not be the end. Eternity must needs go on and on, tho there were never an event or thought to mark its movement. There cannot be an end.

They err, not measuring the import of their own arguments, who tell us, in that pride of not-knowing which is so high uplifted beyond any pride of knowledge, that the very form of the word infinite marks it as the sign of a thing inconceivable, being a mere negation. Nay, verily, it is the word end, limit, cessation, that is the negative word, having no meaning except as the negation of continuance; and infinite is the negation of this negation—a thing positive, affirmative, real.

So, then, it is not the idea of infinity to which the human mind is unfitted. The mind is so made that it cannot help receiving that. The incredible, inconceivable idea is the idea of absolute end. So far is the idea of infinity from being inconceivable, that it is just impossible to thrust the conception out of the mind. And with the conception of eternity, there rushes into the thoughtful spirit at once, the awful and lovely conception of "that high and lofty One who inhabiteth eternity, whose name is Holy." By such a wonder of creation is it, that He who made the little ball of the human eye so that it can take in the heavens and the earth, has made the petty intellect of man so that it can take in the knowledge of the infinite God.

II. But, secondly, it is even a greater wonder than this, that the infinite God, whom the intellect has conceived, draws near for a more intimate society with His creature, and enters the heart of man through the gateway of his affections. I say a greater wonder; for it must be confest that this ideal of the intellect, this center in which all infinite attributes inhere, does by His very majesty so overawe the heart that we shrink away from Him. By every new perfection of His nature, that grows upon our apprehension; by His awful power as the Almighty; by His perfect knowledge as the All-wise; by His unswerving steadfastness as the Faithful and True—the Immutable; by the very infinitude of His nature, He is withdrawn farther and farther from the possibility of being counted among those humble objects on which the tendrils of a human heart are able to lay hold. How, for instance, shall this Inhabitant of eternity, whose name is Holy, be well-pleased with His petty creature who has dared withstand His perfect law, and looks shrinking toward the throne of infinite Majesty, fearing and crying, "Unclean! unclean!" How shall any prayer that we can frame bring arguments to bear upon the Mind that knows the end from the beginning, and to whom there is not a word upon our lips, but lo! He knoweth it altogether? How can any pitiful plight into which we may fall move the compassion of Him who is immutable, and under whose benign government even the pains and severities that befall His creatures are wrought into a plan of common beneficence to the whole?

These are questions which the awe-struck intellect, gazing upward at the infinite attributes that adorn the name which is holy, puts to the yearning heart, which, with all the craving of its love, with all the outstretching of its need, gropes after a God to worship, to love, to pray to, if haply it may find Him. And the heart cannot answer back the intellect with arguments of language. But love contains more reason than many arguments; and the strong instincts of affection and devotion with which the humble and contrite heart reaches out after the love and personal friendship of an infinite Creator are themselves an argument that God will not refuse Himself to the affections which He has Himself implanted. The hunger and thirst of our hearts for God are a promise from Him that they shall be filled. He cannot deny Himself.

The very arguments by which we climb to the knowledge of the infinite Spirit are like mountains that separate us from any relation with him of childlike prayer and mutual love. But a trustful confidence can say to these mountains, "Be ye removed and be ye cast into the sea," and it shall be done.

Have you ever pondered that dark mystery of human nature, the origin of the frightful idolatries of India? It seems to be proved that they had their beginning, not (as the prepossessions of modern science would suggest) through development from some form of fetishism baser and coarser still, but by degradation from the most refined and abstract speculations on the infinity, the spirituality, and the immutability of God. No subtler metaphysics is taught to-day in the lecture-rooms of Yale and Princeton than was taught long centuries ago by Hindoo sages, enthroning their supreme divinity in the everlasting, impassive repose of the unconditioned, far beyond the reach of affection, sympathy or prayer, until the needy millions cried out, stifling, famishing, "Give us a God to love, to worship, to pray to!" and, for lack of answer, betook them to the forest or the quarry or the mine, to the carver and the smith, and made them gods that were no gods. So little can argument and reason hold us back in times when the stress of life comes down upon us, and the cravings of the soul grow strong!

I am bringing to the altar of God my offering—my poor little offering of thankfulness and prayer. Here have I my little bundle of anxieties, cares, troubles,—it may be the concerns of a nation in fear and perplexity; it may be the distress and terror of some sorely afflicted little household; it may be the secret of bitterness of some humble and contrite spirit; in any case, a matter how infinitely small when measured by the scale of immensity and eternity; but oh, how great a thing to me! And there meets me, in the way, a philosopher. "And what, forsooth,

have you there? Show it me, now." And I
unroll before Him my little bundle of griefs,
of cares, of pains, of sickness, of fears, of
forebodings,—here a handful of myrrh from
a troubled heart, and there a sprig of frankin-
cense from a grateful spirit. "And this, then,
is what you would bring to lay before the
infinite, the eternal, the omniscient, the unchangeable God!" And each great title smites
upon my heart with discouragement and
dismay. "This is what you would bring to
Him in prayer and deprecation! But do you
not know that all this is a part of a perfect
system?—that it is all fixt by the laws of
nature, which no prayer can change or suspend without upsetting the constitution of
the universe. You would lay before God your
wretched plight to move His pity? Tush!
Did He not know it all a hundred thousand
ages ago, or ever the earth was?" And I cannot gainsay Him, and I cannot cease to pray.
But by and by the philosopher himself comes
face to face with some of the overwhelming
things in human life and human death. He
hangs with tears and wringing of hands over
some cradleful of childish anguish, and
shrinks from what the laws of nature, the
system of the universe, are doing there—so
pitiless, so deaf to prayer, so blind to agony;
and he looks away, and looks up, and cries,
"My God, my God!" And his reason is not
one whit the less true, because now, at last,

his love and faith are also true and strong. The awful wonder of God's unchangeable infinity abides; but out of cloud and darkness breaks forth, oh, what light of fatherly love! And the bewildered soul sings:—

> And can this mighty King
>   Of glory condescend?
> And will He write His name
>   My Father, and my Friend?
> I love His name! I love His word!
> Join all my powers and praise the Lord!

And now behold a mystery—the mystery of godliness, without controversy great, manifest in the flesh! That He may come over these mountains of helpless separation, that we may be helped to know, to love, to trust that which is far too vast for the reach of our clinging affections to clasp, what wonders of condescending tenderness will not our Father do! There draweth near to us One having the likeness of man, but glorious with an unearthly glory, as of the only-begotten of the Father, full of grace and truth. He stands beside us in our daily cares, our household joys and griefs, our business troubles and anxieties, our national fears and sorrows. He shares our temptations. He is touched with the feeling of our infirmities. He carries our sorrows. He bears our sickness. He dies our death. How easy to love Him, to come near to Him, to trust Him! Being lifted up, how doth

He draw all men unto Him! And what mean those wonderful words of His, telling of His intimacy, His sonship, His oneness with the invisible and eternal God? Could it be, perhaps, that such an one might bring us nearer to the inaccessible Light—might help us to draw nigh as seeing Him who is invisible? Oh, Master, show us the Father and it sufficeth us! And hear now His gracious words: "He that believeth on me believeth on him that sent me." "He that hath seen me hath seen the Father also." Thus the high and lofty One, who hath wonderfully entered into our narrow understanding, cometh also into our heart, and draweth us to His own bosom "with the chords of love, with the bands of a man."

III. Finally, with a true spiritual intercourse and converse, which no man can define, which is as the viewless wind that men know altho they see it not, and feel its quickening and refreshment, altho they cannot tell whence it cometh nor whither it goeth, God entereth into our spirits, "not to sojourn, but to abide with us," and we become the temples of the Holy Ghost.

THE WORLD'S GREAT SERMONS

BIOGRAPHICAL NOTE

JOSEPH PARKER

A WORD TO THE WEARY

BIOGRAPHICAL NOTE

JOSEPH PARKER was born at Hexham-on-Tyne, England, in 1830. He was a prodigious worker, writer, and preacher. His "The People's Bible," in twenty-eight large volumes, a popular commentary on the Scriptures, is his greatest work. To a naturally energetic personality he added great originality and resourcefulness. He gave much time to the preparation of sermons, reading them aloud as he wrote in order to test their effect upon the ear. A strong personal quality pervaded all his preaching. "If I have not seen Him myself," he said, "I cannot preach Him." In lectures to students he gave much valuable advice gathered from the storehouse of his own varied experience. He gave particular attention to the use of the voice. "It is not enough," he said, "that you be heard; you must be effective as well as audible; you must lighten and thunder with the voice; it must rise and fall like a storm at times; now a whisper, now a trumpet, now the sound of many waters. There is an orator's voice, and there is a bellman's. The auctioneer talks; the orator speaks." Dr. Parker's sermons are published in numerous volumes. He died in 1902.

JOSEPH PARKER

1830—1902

A WORD TO THE WEARY [1]

The Lord God hath given me the tongue of the learned,
that I should know how to speak a word in season to
him that is weary.—Isaiah l., 4.

THE power of speaking to the weary is
nothing less than a divine gift. As
we see the divinity in our gifts shall
we be careful of them, thankful for them:
every gift seems to enshrine the giver, God.
But how extraordinary that this power of
speaking to the weary should not be taught
in the schools. It is not within the ability of
man to teach other men how to speak to the
weary-hearted, the wounded in spirit, the sore
in the innermost feelings of the being. But
can we lay down directions about this and
offer suggestions? Probably so, but we do
not touch the core of the matter. There is
an infinite difference between the scholar and
the genius. The scholar is made, the genius
is inspired. Information can be imparted,
but the true sense, the sense that feels and
sees God, is a gift direct from heaven.

[1] From "The People's Bible," by Joseph Parker,
published by Funk & Wagnalls Company.

It is a common notion that anybody can sing. Why can you sing? Why, because I have been taught. That is your mistake. You can sing mechanically, exactly, properly, with right time, right tune, but really and truly you can not sing. Here is a man with his music and with the words; he sings every note, pronounces every word, goes through his lesson, finishes his task, and nobody wants to hear him any more. Another man takes up the same music, the same words, and the same hearers exclaim, "Oh, that he would go on for ever!" How is that?—the words exactly the same, the notes identical—how? Soul, fire, ever-burning, never consuming, making a bush like a planet. The great difficulty in all such cases is the difficulty of transferring to paper a proper or adequate conception of the power of the men who thus sway the human heart. There are some men whose biographies simply belie them, and yet every sentence in the biography is true in the letter; but the biography is little else than a travesty and a caricature, because the power was personal, it was in the face, in the voice, in the presence, in the gait, in the touch—an incommunicable power; the hem of the garment trembled under it, but no biographer could catch it in his scholarly ink.

Very few ministers can enter a sick chamber with any probability of doing real and lasting good. They can read the Bible, and they can pray, and yet, when they have gone, the room seems as if they had never been there. There is no sense of emptiness or desolation. Other men, probably not so much gifted in some other directions, will enter the sick room, and there will be a light upon the wall, summer will gleam upon the windowpane, and angels will rustle in the air, and it will be a scene of gladness and a vision of triumph. How is that? The Lord God hath given me the tongue of the learned that I might know how—*how* to speak a word in season to him that is weary. The Lord God hath not only given me a word to say, but hath given me learning to teach me how to speak it. Place the emphasis upon the how, and then you develop all the mystery, all the tender music, all the infinite capacity of manner.

We may say the right word in the wrong tone; we may preach the gospel as if it were a curse. The common notion is that anybody can go into the Sunday-school and teach the young. We sometimes think that it would be well if a great many persons left the Sunday-school all over the world. Teach the young—would God I had that great gift, to break the bread for the children, and to be able to lure and captivate opening minds, and to enter into the spirit of the words—

"Delightful task! to rear the tender thought,
To teach the young idea how to shoot."

It requires to be father and mother and sister and nurse and genius to speak to the young. They may hear you and not care for you: they may understand your words, and be repelled by your spirit. You require the tongue of the learned to know how to speak, and that tongue of the learned is not to be had at school, college, university—it is not included in any curriculum of learning—it is a gift divine, breathing an afflatus, an inspiration—the direct and distinct creation of God, as is the star, the sun. The speaker, then, is Jesus Christ, the Son of God, the representative of the Father, the incarnate Deity—He it is who is charged with the subtle learning; He it is whose lips tremble with the pathos of this ineffable music.

Tho the gift itself is divine, we must remember that it is to be exercised seasonably. The text is, "that I should know how to speak a word in season." There is a time for everything. It is not enough to speak the right word, it must be spoken at the right moment. Who can know when that is! We can not be taught. We must feel it, see it hours beyond: nay, must know when to be silent for the whole twenty-four hours and to say, "To-morrow, at such and such a time, we will drop that sentence upon the listening ear." "The day after to-morrow, he will probably be in circumstances to admit of this communication being delivered with sympathy and effect."

How few persons know the right time—the right time in conversation. Some people are never heard in conversation tho they are talking all the time. They talk so unseasonably, they talk when other people are talking; they can not wait; they do not know how to come in along the fine line of silence: they do not understand the German expression "Now an angel has passed," and they do not quickly enough follow in his wake. Consequently, tho chattering much they are saying nothing— tho their words be multitudinous, the impression they make is a blank.

I have a ripe seed in my hand. As an agriculturist I am going to sow it. Any laborer in the field can tell me that I should be acting foolishly in sowing it just now. Why? "It is out of season," the man says. "There is a time for the doing of that action: I will tell you when the time returns—do it then, and you may expect a profitable result of your labor."

Then I will change the character and be a nurse, and I will attend to my patient (perhaps I will over attend to him—some patients are killed by over nursing), and I will give the patient this medicine—it is the right medicine. So it is, but you are going to give it at the wrong time, and if you give the medicine at the wrong time, tho itself be right, the hour being wrong you will bring suffering upon the patient, and you yourself will be involved in pains and penalties. Thus we touch that very subtle and sensitive line in human life, the line of refined discrimination. You may say "I am sure I told him." You are right—you did tell him and he did not hear you. You may reply, "I am perfectly confident I delivered the message,—I preached the exact words of the gospel." So you did, but you never got the hearing heart, your manner was so unsympathetic, so ungentle, so cruel (not meant to be—unconsciously so), that the man never understood it to be a gospel. You spoilt the music in the delivery, in the giving of the message. The Lord God giveth the tongue of the learned, that he to whom it is given may know how to speak—how to speak the right word—how to speak the right word at the right point of time. You want divine teaching in all things, in speech not least.

This is a curious word to find in the Bible. Does the Bible care about weary people? We have next to no sympathy with them. If a man be weary, we give him notice to quit: if he ask us to what place he can retire, we tell him that it is his business not ours. Now the tenderness of this Book is one of the most telling, convincing arguments on behalf of its inspiration, and its divine authority. This Book means to help us, wants to help us, it says, "I will try to help you, never hinder you: I will wait for you, I will soften the wind into a whisper, I will order the thunder to be silent, I will quiet the raging sea; I will wait upon you at home, in solitude, at midnight, anywhere—fix the place, the time, yourself, and when your heart most needs me I will be most to your heart.'' Any book found in den, in gutter, that wants to do this, should be received with respect. The purpose is good: if it fail, it fails in a noble object.

Everywhere in this Book of God we find a supreme wish to help man. When we most need help the words are sweeter than the honeycomb. When other books are dumb, this Book speaks most sweetly. It is like a star, it shines in the darkness, it waits the going down of the superficial sun of our transient prosperity, and then it breaks upon us as the shadows thicken. This is the real greatness of God: he will not break the bruised reed. Because the reed is bruised, therefore the rude man says he may break it. His argument in brief is this: ''If the reed were strong, I should not touch it, but seeing that it is bruised what harm can there be in completing the wound under which it is already suffering? I will even snap it and throw the sundered parts away.'' That is the reasoning of the rude man—that is the vulgar view of the case. The idea of the healing is the idea of a creator. He who creates also heals. Herein we see God's estimate of human nature: if He cared only for the great, the splendid, the magnificent, the robust, and the everlasting, then

He would indeed be too like ourselves. The greatness of God and the estimate which He places upon human nature are most seen in all these ministrations in reference to the weak and the weary and the young and the feeble and the sad. Made originally in the image of God, man is dear to his Maker, tho ever so broken. Oh, poor prodigal soul with the divinity nearly broken out of thee, smashed, bleeding, crushed, all but in hell— while there is a shadow of thee outside perdition, He would heal thee and save thee. Thou art a ruin, but a grand one,—the majestic ruin of a majestic edifice, for knowest thou not that thou wast the temple of God?

When we are weary, even in weariness, God sees the possibility of greatness that may yet take place and be developed and supervene in immortality. How do we talk? Thus: "The survival of the fittest." It is amazing with what patience and magnanimity and majestic disregard of circumstances we allow people to die off. When we hear that thousands have perished, we write this epitaph on their white slate tombstones: "The survival of the fittest required the decay of the weakest and the poorest." We pick off the fruit which we think will not come to perfection. The gardener lays his finger and thumb upon the tree, and he says, "This will not come to much"— he wrenches the poor unpromising piece of fruit off the twig and throws it down as useless. In our march we leave the sick and wounded behind. That is the great little, the majestic insignificant, the human contradiction. We go in for things that are fittest, strongest, most promising, healthy, self-complete, and therein we think we are wise. God says, "Not a lamb must be left out—bring it up: not a sick man must be omitted: not a poor publican sobbing his 'God be merciful to me a sinner' must be omitted from the great host. Bring them all in, sick, weary, wounded, feeble, young, illiterate, poor, insignificant, without name, fame, station, force —all in: gather up the fragments that nothing be lost." Let us go to that Shepherd— He will spare us and love us. When our poor strength gives out, He will not set His cruel heel upon us and kill us, He will gather us in His arms and make the whole flock stand still till He has saved the weakest one.

Did we but know the name for our pain we should call it Sin. What do we need, then, but Christ the Son of God, the Heart of God, the Love of God? He will in very deed give us rest. He will not add to the great weight which bows down our poor strength. He will give us grace, and in His power all our faintness shall be thought of no more. Some of us know how dark it is when the full shadow of our sin falls upon our life, and how all the help of earth and time and man does but mock the pain it can not reach. Let no man say that Christ will not go so low down as to find one so base and vile as he. Christ is calling for thee; I heard His sweet voice lift itself up in the wild wind and ask whither thou hadst fled, that He might save thee from death and bring thee home. There is no wrath in His face or voice, no sword is swung by His hand as if in cruel joy, saying, "Now at last I have My chance with you." His eyes gleam with love: His voice melts in pity: His words are gospels, every one. Let Him but see thee sad for sin, full of grief because of the wrong thou hast done, and He will raise thee out of the deep pit and set thy feet upon the rock.

McKENZIE

THE ROYAL BOUNTY

BIOGRAPHICAL NOTE

ALEXANDER MCKENZIE was born at New
Bedford, Mass., in 1830, and graduated
from Harvard in 1859. Since 1867 he has
been pastor of the First Congregational
Church, Cambridge, Mass. His voice is
rich, full and sympathetic, and his pulpit
style that of one man talking earnestly
and directly to another, there being no attempt at oratorical effect. He is to-day
probably the most acceptable preacher at
Harvard, and the leading Congregational
minister in New England. The discourse
reprinted here is from his volume "A
Door Opened," and has been noted as one
of the greatest sermons of the century.

McKENZIE

BORN IN 1830

THE ROYAL BOUNTY[1]

*And King Solomon gave to the Queen of Sheba all
her desire, whatsoever she asked, besides that which
Solomon gave her of his royal bounty. So she turned
and went to her own land, she and her servants.*—1
Kings x., 13.

THE Queen of Sheba came from the uttermost part of the earth to hear the
wisdom of Solomon. She was amazed
at all that she had heard, and delighted with
all that she saw, and confest that after the
generous rumors that had reached her in her
distant home the half had not been told her.
She brought her present to him, as was the
custom of the times; and when she went away
she asked a gift of him, and history says that
the king gave her all that she desired; and
that, having given her everything of which she
had thought, he added something more of his
own thought. He gave her this, not because
she had desired it, but because he had desired
it; not for her heart's seeking, but out of his
heart's wishing to bestow. This is the simple

[1] Reprinted by permission of Dr. Alexander McKenzie and the publishers, Houghton, Mifflin Co.

211

record: "And King Solomon gave to the Queen of Sheba all her desire, whatsoever she asked, besides that which Solomon gave her of his royal bounty." These last words describe the added gift, and this was doubtless the best of all; that upon which she would think with the greatest pleasure, and of which she would speak with the greatest pride. The word "royal" is well chosen, for we think of something which is great when we apply this term to it, as we speak of a royal deed, royal magnificence, royal benevolence, royal bounty. We readily approve the action of the king, for it is this excess of giving, beyond that which is demanded of us, which makes the real generosity. We are in the habit ourselves, so far as we are generous at all, of reaching beyond the real necessities and requests of our friends, and giving out of the largeness of our hearts. It is this excess which commands the high price. It is the added, extraordinary beauty of a painting which enhances its worth. Some pictures are sold by the square yard, and some by the inch. It is that which genius adds which is the royal bounty. It marks the difference between genius and talent. To be what we must, and to do what we must, is narrow and uninteresting. The man who is just, and no more, wins our praise for his integrity, but not our regard for his liberality. There are some men who would on no account have their measures in the slightest degree too small, but would be

quite as careful not to have them too large.
There is no reason why justice should not be
combined with charity, and a strict regard for
the legal demands which are made upon us
with the excess out of a free heart which will
make our justice beautiful. I saw in a fine
country town a tall, graceful tree which cast
its pleasant shade upon the path, and I
marked that men had fastened upon it an
iron frame which held a lamp that gave out
its light upon the path. The tree was not
the less a tree that it added the light, and
the lamp was not less a lamp because it be-
longed to the tree. I came afterward and
found that the bark of the tree had grown up
around the iron where it was fastened to it,
till the frame and lamp were fairly incorporated in the tree itself. It is easy thus to
enlarge our life, adding beauty to strength,
giving what our heart desires to give to that
which Sheba asks at our hands. This thought
is strongly expressed by St. Paul, ''Scarcely
for a righteous man,'' the man who does exactly what he ought to do, and nothing more,
''will one die.'' Yet peradventure, for a
good man, who does all he ought to do, and
adds something because he wants to do it, some
would even give their life. This man appeals
to our heart which is ready to respond. The
best things are indeed only to be given in this
way. They can not be bought. They can not
be had for the asking; such things as con-

fidence, and friendship, and courtesy, which no statute can demand, but which the royal heart delights to give; and there is a like royalty which is able to receive and prize the gift.

This is God's way, to whom all life is but the expression of his heart. We rejoice continually in his bountiful goodness. What is the need of flowers? He could have made a strong and honest earth which would take in the seed and give it out in harvest, and thus we could live; but when He had made the earth substantial, useful as it is, He added flowers, because He wished to give them, was delighted to look upon them, and knew how happy we should be who saw them blossom by the roadside. There is no need of birds. The world would go its way, the seasons would follow one another, the sun would rise and set, the forest trees would reach up toward the clouds, without them. God made all this, and then filled the quiet woods with forms of beauty, and changed silence into songs. Even heaven itself has more than we should have looked for or asked for. We might have had a good delightful heaven, without pain or sorrow or sighing, without death, and such a heaven we have. But in the vision of the Apocalypse, which only dimly sees the heavenly reality, its streets are covered with gold, as it were transparent glass; its gates are pearl, and the strong walls, which can not be

moved, glisten with jewels. So it might have
been with the arrangement of this world. We
might have had men to care for us, women
to nurture us, fathers to work for us, a society
whose process might move on with industry
and safety from year to year. But God has
added the richer delights of love and sympathy, of all that we name friend and friendship. It is in the same way that He frames
His ordinances for us. We could have had all
days alike, but when He had made six good
days He added a seventh which should be
wearied by no work, wherein the soul should
be at leisure to live with itself in quietness,
and worship God. He might have supplied
all our wants in the course of nature, bringing
His gifts to our door with regularity, and we
should have lived our appointed time; but He
does more than this. He lets us thank Him
when we take our daily bread, and blesses
the bread with the love which gives it. He
even lets us tell Him what we wish, and to
our wishes He gives patient heed. He might
have left us to conscience and experience, in
the light of nature to frame our character
and our hope, but to these He has added the
thought of other men, the revelation of His
wisdom by His saints, the gift of His spirit to
our spirit, to be in us a continual light.

There is a very good expression of God's
way of dealing with us in a line of the twenty-
third Psalm, "My cup runneth over." This

seems unnecessary. To have the cup full, or
a little less than full, is enough for us, and
more convenient. For us, but not for God,
who delights in filling it; and when we bid
Him stay His hand, He keeps on pouring, and
the water flows, till, presently, the cup is
overflowing, but not because we thought to
have it so, but because of His great delight in
giving; until it would seem as if He could not
stop, or content Himself with that which He
has already bestowed upon us. Let this stand
as a simple expression of His way with us.

When we come upon anything that all good
men approve, we may be very certain that we
have found something which God Himself ap-
proves, and which is the method of His life.
We like, among ourselves, this principle of the
cup that runneth over. Our liking for it we
have inherited from God. We might expect,
therefore, that when the Son of God has His
life in the world He will live by this rule,
which is of heaven and of earth; and it is even
so. His first miracle would seem unnecessary.
There have been people who blindly but hon-
estly wished that He had never wrought it.
Why did He do it if there was no need of it,
if it were even possible that it should be
wrested from its meaning? He had gone as
a guest to a wedding, perhaps because the
bride was his friend, and there came that
grave calamity which would mar the feast; for
presently it was whispered to Him, "They

have no wine." Surely they could have a wedding without wine. Not that wedding. Not in the custom of that time. He knew that the bride, if she lived to be old, would never recover from the shame of her wedding-day, whose beauty was lost. Here was a necessity, in love, in kindness; and that the cheeks of this girl might not redden with shame, He reddened the water into wine.

He was at Capernaum. They brought to Him a sick man with the palsy. They broke up the roof, and lowered him to the feet of Jesus, who knew well what they wanted. He passed over the little thing which they sought, and, governed by His own feeling, not by theirs, he said, "Son, be of good cheer; thy sins are sent away from thee." That was enough. In a few days, the man would be able to walk without His help. Death comes to the succor of cripples. The man gave no sign of discontent, but Jesus found that the friends were unsatisfied, and He thought within Himself, "You brought him here that he might be raised up, and be made able to carry his bed home. I have done a greater thing for him, but I will add this which you want." "Arise," He said, "take up your bed and go your way." He did the greater work which made the soul strong, and for the lesser work, —well, He threw that in. It was the royal bounty. There was a time later than that, after His resurrection, when some of His disciples had toiled all the night upon the sea, and had taken nothing. He could not have it a fruitless night for them. In the morning He was their risen Savior, who might well bestow some spiritual gift becoming to the resurrection. This He did, but He said, "Cast your net on the right side of the ship, and you will find what you have been seeking." They cast it, therefore, and drew it in, full of fishes, a hundred and fifty and three. This is the record of a fisherman, who wrote that the fish were large; and of an old man, who remembered the number of them. They drew their net to shore, and there was a fire of coals, and fish laid thereon, another fish. When they had enough, one that was better than all was added. Have you not sometimes wished that you could have had that hundred and fifty-fourth fish? This was Christ's way all the while, and is His way still. He fills the net as full as it will hold, that our life may be sustained, and then He adds more, that His love may be gratified, and that which He adds is the "royal bounty."

The work of our Lord was not merely in meeting the wants of men, but in creating the wants; not in gratifying their great desires, but in making their desires great. His own work in the world was twofold: to teach men how much more there was which they could enjoy, and how much more there was which He was eager to impart. The greater

the desire, the surer it was that it would be
met by His desire. Indeed, a large desire is
necessary to wealth. We must look out toward
that wherein our riches lie. "He who would
bring home the wealth of the Indies must
send out the wealth of the Indies." To him
whose desires are allowed liberty there comes
the answer of fulfillment from "the unsearchable riches of Christ." In all His life and in
all His teachings we see vastly more than men
ever asked, much more than they are willing
to take even to-day. It has often been, as it
was at the first, that "he came unto his
own, and his own received him not"; but
to those who received Him He gave all they
wished, and more than they had thought; He
gave the right to become the sons of God.
They would have been content with a greater
prophet, a bolder leader, a stronger king, a
Messiah who should enthrone Israel and bring
the nations in homage to its feet. He came
bringing God to the world, giving an eternal
liberty, erecting an everlasting kingdom.
They wanted manna; He gave the bread of
life. They wanted wells of water; He gave
the well that should be within them, springing
up for evermore. They wanted a leader; He
gave a Savior. They wanted man; and He
was God. This has continued even to our
time. Many admire Christ because He was
a teacher, neglecting that wherein He was infinitely more than teacher. They are glad of

an example; He was that, but, far beyond it, He was the life whereby righteousness became possible. There are those who would be content with His beautiful spirit, His blameless life, His deeds of charity, His patience, His submission, His consent to a death which He could not avoid. He offers to the world the spirit of the Eternal, the life of God to be lived upon the earth; He lays down the life which no man could take from Him; and, with all the roads leading from Jerusalem open before Him, walks with determined step to Calvary and the cross. Beyond that which has contented many in the world, He gave Himself, the world's Redeemer, the Lamb of God, the Good Shepherd giving His life for the sheep.

It is very, very sad to mark how ready we are to measure Christ's gifts to us by our narrow wants and limited desires; not by the greatness of His love, not by His exhaustless riches, not by the fulness of the grace of the Eternal, who is the Father and friend of all men. If ever we shall pass beyond the gratifying of ourselves, and allow Christ to gratify Himself in blessing us, we shall find in a glad experience what the simple words mean, "I am come that they might have life"—oh, friends, do not stop there, finish the sentence, —"I am come that they might have life, and that they might have it more abundantly." We ask life of Him, and He gives us life, and offers length of days forever and forever. We pray that we may live; and we set up a goal at seventy or ninety years, when He draws no line across our path. "I give eternal life," He says. We pray for help that we may live; He offers more than that in the unrivaled sentence, "Because I live, ye shall live also." We think of life as being, and are content. We use existence as a synonym of living, but He said, "This is eternal life, to know God, and me."

So for ourselves; we are to live as His disciples. We wish to be true, useful, and generous. We wish to do in small measure such things as He did,—in His name to give the cup of water, and the healing of the sick. He grants all that we desire, then speaks out of His own heart, and His desire, "The works that I do shall ye do, and greater works than these"; for the miracles which attract us or baffle us, which draw us to His love, or possibly turn us from His word, which are only miracles because they are strange to us, are to be exceeded in the things which we do, when by our teaching we open the eyes of men that they may see God, and lift them up to the ways of holy living, and raise them from being into life. Our visions of heaven in our reverent imagination, even in the exultant words of the Revelation, are not equal to the simple truths which He taught, and men learned to repeat after Him. For what are golden streets and jeweled walls beside that which He meant, "In my Father's house are many mansions." "I go to prepare a place for you." "Ye shall behold my glory." "Ye shall be loved as I am loved." The thought of Christ far outruns the aspiration of the world, as it comes to us from the lips of that disciple whom Jesus loved, "We shall be like him, for we shall see him even as he is."

What do we need, then? To enlarge our desires! Yes, but to consent to God's desires. To wish for more, but to consent to be blest as Christ longs to bless us. We must know the methods of God, whose will to give is greater and more constant than our will to receive. We must adjust our life to God's desire. Faith is the compact of the soul with God, rather than with itself. "Open thy mouth wide, and I will fill it," is a promise ever old and ever new. We must be firm enough and aspiring enough to hold the cup after it has begun to overflow, and to let God's hand pour the water of life as long as He will, for this world and all the worlds that are to be. If we could desire more, if we could ascend to God's desire for us, life would be transfigured.

"The balsam, the wine, of predestinate wills
  Is a jubilant longing and pining for God."

"God loves to be longed for, He loves to be sought,
  For He sought us Himself, with such longing and
    love."

We wish now to take this method for our
own in all our dealing with God. Our sense
of what is right, the voice of conscience, the
commands of Scripture, call us to our duty.
Let us do what they require till conscience is
satisfied; but let us add to this more than a
rigid obedience asks for, all that a loving
heart, grateful and generous, wishes to bestow.
The little questions of life, small matters of
casuistry, minute affairs of conduct, would be
quite readily determined if we would live by
this rule, wherewith God blesses us. That
question which with unusual urgency now
presses upon us, how we shall regard the Sabbath day, would not be difficult if it were our
delight to remember it, and to keep it holy because it is our delight to please Him who has
given to us its sacredness and blessedness. It
is pitiful when we find ourselves questioning
how much of the day should be holy; how
much of it should be given to the thought of
God and the divine life; how much of it we
should yield to the holy spirit of truth; how
many of the hours we should keep in the re-
membrance of Him whose resurrection gives
to the Sabbath its greater meaning. We
should keep the Sabbath holy as if we desired
to keep it holy. All its hours should be sacred.
They need not be less joyous, less friendly, for
being holy; and we can not be gratified with
the spirit in which we find ourselves trying to
divide the time. Keep twenty-four hours for

God, and if by any means you can make the time overflow add a twenty-fifth hour.

We question again about money. What proportion of our property should we devote to God? The Jews said one-tenth. Can we do no better, after so long a time? Let us give the whole, and if by any means we can compass it, let us add another tenth, simply to show what a delight it is to give all things to Him, and to let Him make the allotment in His care for us, and for our household, and for the Church, and for the wide world that we are living in. There are many who do this, and they learn how true is that word of Christ that is called to mind among the Acts of the Apostles, "It is more blessed to give than to receive."

Thus, in all things let us make the way of God our own, become His children entirely, receive the love of Christ in its fulness, make up our own life in His name, according to the largeness of His thought. If we will consent to it, we can be great and rich and strong. It seems strange to say that we are not ready to be blest, but of many it is true. They are not willing to be greatly blest, to have the cup run over. They are willing to be useful, but not very useful. They ask to be set in His service, but when He takes their word and breathes His own desire into it, they shrink back. It is a very serious thing, if we are able to perceive it, to consent that God should bless us as He pleases, should have His own estimate of our character, His own measure of our powers, His own vision of our accomplishment, and should call us to greater service, to diviner employment, than we have ever dreamed of. It was a wise woman who said, "I have had to face my own prayers." We face our prayers when God gives His own wish to our words, and makes them large enough to hold His thoughts. It is one of the hardest things to believe, but one to which, in humbleness of mind and in a faith which will not falter, we should consent,—that high word of calling and consecration which Christ gave more than once,—"As the Father hath sent me into the world, even so send I you." Not our thought but His thought makes our calling, and the thought of God is the summons and the guidance of our life. Even so, even according to Thy greatness, and Thy gentleness which makes men great; Thine infinite purposes, and Thine eternal grace; even so, O Lord of mercy and of truth, send us into the world!

As we close these thoughts, let us remember that promise which comes at the close of the Old Testament, which almost seems to reverse the promise at the beginning of the Old Testament, "I will never open the windows of heaven and pour out a flood again"; for the last of the prophets brings to us the word of God, that He will open the windows of heaven, and pour out a flood again. It shall not come to destroy, but to preserve; it shall create life; it shall enlarge life, but it shall be after the measure of His will, not ours. "Bring ye all the tithes into the storehouse, and prove me now herewith, if I will not open the windows of heaven, and pour out a blessing that there shall not be room enough to receive it." Not drops here and there, but showers of blessing. Not running brooks, but broad rivers. Not pools of water, but a shoreless sea; deep, deep waters, when, looking up into the infinite Love, and consenting to be blest of God as God would bless us, we bring all the tithes into the storehouse and the remainder of the tithes, if any have been left. "I will pour you out a blessing, that there shall not be room enough to receive it." Not room enough to receive it; that is the royal bounty.

FARRAR

WORK IN THE GROANING CREATION

BIOGRAPHICAL NOTE

FREDERICK WILLIAM FARRAR was born in Bombay, India, in 1831. He was educated at King's College, London, and at Trinity College, Cambridge. He became dean of Canterbury in 1895, and died in 1903. His Life of Christ, the most widely read of his many religious works, has been translated into many languages—even into Japanese. The following illustrates his power of emphasis.

"There, amid those voluptuous splendors, Pilate, already interested, already feeling in this prisoner before him some nobleness which touched his Roman nature, asking Him in pitying wonder, 'Art thou the King of the Jews?'—Thou poor, worn, tear-stained outcast, in this hour of Thy bitter need—O pale, lonely, friendless, wasted man, in Thy poor peasant garments, with Thy tied hands and the foul traces of the insults of Thine enemies on Thy face and on Thy robes—Thou, so unlike the fierce, magnificent Herod, whom this multitude which thirsts for Thy blood acknowledged as their sovereign—art Thou the King of the Jews?"

FARRAR

1831—1903

WORK IN THE GROANING CREATION [1]

And God saw everything that he had made, and behold it was very good.—Gen. i., 31.

For we know that the whole creation groaneth and travaileth in pain together until now.—Rom. viii., 22.

And there shall be no more curse.—Rev. xxii., 3.

IN those three texts you have the past, the present, the future of our earth; what was, what is, what shall be; the perfectness which man has marred, the punishment which he is enduring, the hope to which he looks. What share we may have in the marring or the mending of this our transitory dwelling, that is our main subject to-day.

We see some glimpses at least of the truth that actively by sympathy, by thoughtfulness, by charity, by unselfishness, by loving one another;—that even passively by abstaining from the fashionable and universal vice of biting and devouring one another;—we see that by honesty, by self-reverence, by reverence for others, by obeying the golden rule of

[1] Reprinted by permission of Messrs. E. P. Dutton & Co.

"doing unto others as we would they should do unto us," we may do very much to limit the realm of sorrow, and to substitute a golden for an iron scepter in its sway over human hearts. We see, too, that our own inevitable trials and humiliations,—all the neglect, all the insult, all the weariness, all the disappointment, all the ingratitude, which may befall us,—can be better borne if we be cheerful and active in doing good. Labor for God is the best cure for sorrow, and the best occupation of life.

Can we to-day push the inquiry yet further, and learn whether it is in our power in any way to mend the flaw which runs for us through the material world; or in any way to diminish for ourselves and for mankind the pressure of that vast weight of laws which exercises over us, undoubtedly, a sway of awful potency? The whole creation groaneth and travaileth in pain together until now; can we—not by any strength of ours, but because God permits and desires it, can we do anything to hasten that blest hour for which we wait—the hour of the new creation; of the adoption, to wit, the redemption of our body; of the restitution of all things; of the *palingenesia* of the world?

I think we can. I know that the supposed helplessness of man is a favorite topic of modern materialism, which makes of man the irresponsible tool of forces which he can not resist, the sport and prey of dumb powers which are alike inexorable and passionless. This philosophy—if we may call it a philosophy—laughs to scorn the notion of a miracle, and makes virtue and vice not the conscious choice of free beings, but the inevitable result of material causes and hereditary impulses, of which in all but semblance, we are the mere automata and slaves. My brethren, into all these speculations of a baseless atheism, I need not enter. To us, nature means nothing but the sum total of phenomena which God has created; and since in the idea of nature is included the idea of God, a miracle becomes as natural and as easily conceivable as the most ordinary occurrence. And we know that we are free, that God does not mock us, that we can abhor that which is evil, and cleave to that which is good. The laws of nature are nothing, then, for us but observed sequences, and we do not admit that there is anything fearful in their uniformity. It is true that nature drives her plowshare straight onwards, and heeds not what may be lying in the furrow; it is true that therefore she shows an apparent indifference to human agony; it is true that if the fairest and sweetest child which earth ever saw be left at play in the face of the advancing tide, the tide will still advance and drown the little life; it is true that the fire in its ruthless vividness will roll over the loveliest maiden whose rich dress should catch its flame. It is a law that resistance must be equal to force, and that if there be a certain amount of pressure of vibration, whatever comes of it, a structure will give way, even though, alas, it hurl nearly a hundred human beings, with one flash of horror, into the gulf of death. But is this any reason for a fierce arraignment of nature, as tho she were execrably ruthless, and execrably indifferent? Not so, my brethren. Death whenever it comes is but death. None of us has any promise of this or that amount of life. It needs no railway accident, no sinking ship, or breaking ice, or burning town, or flame from heaven, or arrow in the darkness, or smiting of the sun by day, or the moon by night, to cut short our days. An invisible sporule in the air may do it, or a lesion no bigger than a pin's point.

"He ate, drank, laughed, loved, lived, and liked life
    well;
Then came—who knows?—some gust of jungle wind,
A stumble on the path; a taint i' the tank;
A snake's nip; half a span of angry steel;
A chill; a fishbone; or a falling tile,—
And life is over, and the man is dead."

But is this any reason why we should look on ourselves as victims of dead irresponsible forces? Why so? Death is but death, and if we live faithfully, death is our richest birthright. "Were you ready to die that you jumped into the stormy sea to save that child's

life?" said a gentleman to an English sailor.
"Should I have been better prepared, sir,"
the sailor answered, "if I had shirked my
duty?" A sudden death is often, and in
many respects, the most merciful form of
death; and the apparently terrible death of
a few may save the lives of many hundreds.
The uniformity of nature may sometimes wear
the aspect of passionless cruelty; but as we
learn more and more to observe and to obey
her laws, we find more and more that they
work for countless ends of beneficence and
beauty, that out of seeming evil she works
real good, out of transient evil enduring good.
The fires which rend the earthquake and burst
from the volcano, are the quickening forces
of the world; her storms lash the lazy atmosphere which otherwise would stagnate into
pestilence, and it is for man's blessing, not
for his destruction, that her waters roll and
her great winds blow.

But are we, after all, so very helpless before
the aggregate of these mighty forces, as materialism loves to represent? Not so! "Thou
madest him to have dominion over the works
of thy hands," said the Psalmist, "Thou hast
put all things under his feet." "Replenish
the earth, and subdue, and have dominion,"
said the first utterance of God to man. And
what is this but an equivalent of the latest
utterances of science, that "the order of nature is ascertainable by our faculties to an

extent which is practically unlimited, and that
our volition counts for something in the
course of events''? Man has done much to
make the world in all senses a worse place for
himself, but he has also, thank God, done
much to make it better, and he may, to an
almost unspeakable extent, remedy for himself and for his race the throes and agonies
of the groaning universe. God meant His
earth to be a more blest place for us than it
is, and in every instance men have made it
more blest when they have read the open secrets, by virtue of which, for our excitement,
if not for our reward, ''herbs have their healing, stones their preciousness, and stars their
times.'' Ancient nations have shuddered at
the awfulness of the sea. It drowns ship and
sailor; but ''trim your sail, and the same
wave which drowns the bark is cleft by it, and
bears it along like its own foam, a plume and
a power.'' The lightning shatters tower and
temple; but once learn that it is nothing but
the luminous all-pervading fluid which you
may evolve by rubbing a piece of amber, and
brush out of a child's fair hair, and then with
no more potent instrument than a boy's kite
you may dash harmless to the earth the all-
shattering brand which was the terror of antiquity; nay, you may seize it by its wing of
fire, and bid it carry your messages around
the girdled globe. Zymotic diseases smite
down the aged and young, but, when you have

learnt that they are caused by myriads of invisible germs which float in the water or the air, you have but to observe the commonest rules of sanitary science, to filter and boil the dangerous water, to insure free currents of air, to breathe as nature meant you to breathe, through the nostrils, and not through the throat, and you rob them of half their deadliness. Why has smallpox been stayed in its loathly ravages, and deprived of its hideous power? Why does the Black Death rage no longer, as it raged among the monks of this Abbey four centuries ago? Why do we not have pestilence, like that great plague of London, which destroyed 7,165 persons in a single week? Why has jail fever disappeared? Why are the cities of Europe horrified no longer by the hideousness of medieval leprosy? Because men live amid cleaner and purer surroundings. Because rushes are no longer strewn over floors which had been suffered to be saturated with the organic refuse of years. Because the simplest laws of nature are better understood. Because, in these respects, men have remedied by God's aid, some of those miseries for which the Savior sighed.

And this amelioration of man's miseries is a great, and noble, and Christlike work. Would that there were no other side to the picture! Man, alas! also has done, and may do, infinite mischief to the world he lives in. He may cut down the forests on the hills, and so diminish the necessary rain. He may pluck up the grasses on the shore, and so lay waste whole acres to the devastating sands. He may poison the sweet, pure rivers of his native soil, till their crystal freshness is corrupted into deathful and putrescent slime. He may herd together, as we suffer our poor to do, in filthy tenements which shall breed every species of disease and vice. He may indulge or acquiesce in senseless fashions and pernicious vanities which shall mean not only wasteful ugliness and grotesque extravagance, but leave shattered health and ruined lives, to the mothers of his race. He may in greed of competition extirpate the game of the forest, the fishes of the sea. He may destroy the exquisite balance of nature, by shooting down or entrapping the sweet birds of the air, till his vines and his harvests are devastated by the insects on which they feed. He may suffer the chimneys of his manufactories to poison the atmosphere with black smoke and sulphurous acid, till his proudest cities are stifled at noonday, as we all have seen in London for these many weeks, with the unclean mirk of midnight fogs. He may suffer noxious gases to be vomited upon the breeze, till the most glorious buildings in his cities corrode and crumble—as the stones of this Abbey are doing—under their influence,—till the green woods blacken into leafless wastes, and life is lived at miserable levels of vitality under the

filthy reek. There is hardly any limit to the
evil, no less than to the good, which man may
do to this his earthly environment. Nor is
it less deplorable that he may go out of his
way to do endless mischief to himself by his
misuse or abuse of the properties of things.
From the dried capsules of the white poppy
he extracts opium, and he grows acres of pop-
pies that with thousands of chests of that
opium he may degrade into decrepitude and
wretchedness the most populous nations upon
earth. Nature gives him the purple grape
and the golden grain, and he mashes them and
lets them rot and seethe, and assists, and su-
perintends, and retards their decomposition,
till he has educed from them a fermented in-
toxicating liquor; and not content with this
luxury, he pours it into Circean cups of degrading excess; not content with even fermen-
tation, he further, by distillation, extracts a
transparent, mobile, colorless fluid, which is
the distinctive element in ardent spirits, and
these, whatever may be their legitimate use in
manufacture or in medicine, he has so horribly
abused that they have become to mankind, the
spiritus ardentes indeed, but not of heaven—
fiery spirits of the abyss, which have deci-
mated nations, ruined continents, shortened
millions of lives, and turned for millions of
God's children, and millions of Christ's little
ones, life into an anguish, and earth into a
hell. Do not say we can do nothing to soften

for man the deadly agencies which are working in the world,—for all this mischief, and incalculably more than this, is man's own doing.

But let me ask you to glance for a moment at one of the beneficent secrets which nature has yielded up to man. Have you ever realized, with heartfelt gratitude to God, the priceless boon which He has granted to this generation in the diminution of pain? One of our best surgeons has just told us the strange yet simple story of this discovery, from the first dim intimation of the possibility in 1789, till in 1846 it might almost be said that in Europe we could name the month, before which all operative surgery was agonizing, and after which it was painless. But what an immense, what an enormous boon is this application of anodynes! "Past all counting is the sum of happiness enjoyed by the millions who have, in the last thirty-three years, escaped the pain that was inevitable in surgical operations; pain made more terrible by apprehension; more keen by close attention; sometimes awful in a swift agony; sometimes prolonged beyond even the most patient endurance, and then renewed in memory, and terrible in dreams. This will never be felt again." And besides this abolition of pain, it would take long to tell how chloroform and ether "have enlarged the field of useful surgery, making many things easy which were difficult, many safe which were perilous, many practical which were nearly impossible." But another lesson this eminent man of science draws, which bears directly on our subject, is that while we are profanely decrying nature, discoveries the most blest, boons the most priceless, may lie close to us and yet God leave us to discover them; and that we may endure many needless miseries, falsely accusing nature and even God, only because we have neither hope enough to excite intense desire, nor desire enough to encourage hope. We wonder that for forty years the discovery of anesthetics was not pursued, tho, after the pregnant hint of Sir H. Davy, it lay but half hidden under so thin a veil. Our successors will wonder at us, as we at those before us, that we were as blind to who can tell how many great truths, which, they will say, were all around us, within reach of any clear and earnest mind. They will wonder at the quietude with which we stupidly acquiesce in, or immorally defend, the causes which perpetuate and intensify our habitual miseries. Our fathers needlessly put up with these miseries "as we now put up with typhoid fever and sea-sickness; with local floods and droughts; with waste of health and wealth in pollutions of rivers; with hideous noises, and foul smells"; with the curse of alcoholic poisoning, and many other miseries. Our successors, when they have remedied or prevented these, will look back on them with horror, and on us with wonder and contempt, for what they will call our idleness or blindness, or indifference to suffering. Alas! in the physical as in the moral world, we murmur at the evils which surround us, and we do not remove them. We multiply those evils, and make life wretched, and then curse nature because it is wretched, and neglect or fling away the precious gifts and easy remedies which would make it blest. And is it not so in the spiritual world? Nine-tenths of our miseries are due to our sins. Yet the remedy of our sins is close at hand. We have a Savior; we have been commemorating His birth, but we live and act as tho He were dead; in our own lives and those of others we suffer those miseries to run riot which He came to cure; we talk and live as tho those remedies were undiscoverable, while from day to day His Word is very nigh us, even in our mouths and in our hearts!

For one sermon you hear about work for the secular amelioration of the suffering world for which Christ sighed, you may (I suppose) hear fifty on passing ecclesiastical controversies and five thousand about individual efforts for personal salvation. And yet one pure, self-sacrificing deed, one word of generosity to an opponent, one kindly act to aid another, may have been better for you in God's sight and far harder for you to do, than to attend in the year the 730 daily services which this Abbey provides. Yes, I am glad that I have preached to you to-day the duty of what some would call secular work—as tho secular work were not often the most profoundly religious work!—for the amelioration of the world. And I say, it were better for you to have made but two blades of grass grow where one grew before, than if, with the hollow, hateful, slanderous heart of some false prophets of modern religionism, you were every morning to do whatever modern thing may be analogous to binding your fringes with blue, and broadening your phylacteries,—to making the hilltops blaze with your sacrificial fires, building here seven altars, and offering a bullock and a ram on every altar. And so, my brethren, let us leave this Abbey to-day with conceptions of duty larger and more hopeful; with more yearning both after the sympathy of Christ and after His activity; with more faith to see that the world would not be so utter a ruin but for our perversity; with more hope to be convinced that even we can help to redeem its disorders, and restore its pristine perfectness. Let us obey the command, "Ephphatha, Be opened!" Let us lift up our eyes to see that, tho the air around us is colorless, the far-off heaven is blue. Let us see and be thankful for the beauty of the world, the sweet air, the sunshine, the sea, the splendid ornaments of heaven, the ever-recurring cir-

cles of the divine beneficence. Let us learn
the secrets of the mighty laws which only
crush us when we disobey them, and which
teach us, with divine inflexibility, that as we
sow we reap. Let us not hinder the students
of science in their patient toil and marvelous
discovery by the crude infallibilities of our
ignorant dogmatism. Let us believe—for we
were saved in hope—that "Utopia itself is but
another word for time"; and that, if our own
work seems but infinitesimal, yet "there are
mites in science, as well as in charity, and the
ultimate results of each are alike important
and beneficial." And so the more we share
in the sigh and in the toil of the Savior, the
more shall we share in His redeeming gladness.

81 4/39